THIS BOOK BELONGS TO:

THE ROWAN STORY BOOK OF
Little Knits

First published in 2007 by
Rowan Yarns
Green Lane Mill
Holmfirth
West Yorkshire
HD9 2DX

Story & concept by Marie Wallin.
Illustrations by Mark Powell.
Photography by Simon Brown.
Styling by Marie Wallin & Sarah Hatton.
Art Direction by Marie Wallin.
Hair & Make up by Charlie Duffy.
Book Layout by Nicky Downes.
Vintage Toys loaned by Les Clarke of Proper Punch, Telephone: 01484 843964.
Models: Max Caddel, Alice Godfrey, Jennifer Faulkner, Edie Hughes and
Alexander Paley – Kids London. Saphira Noor, Daniel Price, Georgina Brunt
and Jasmine Chang Leng – Scallywags.
Location: The Grey House, Chadlington, Oxfordshire – Light Locations
Many thanks to Anna for her kind hospitality and to Barker and Buzz
for being friendly dogs.
Garments knitted by Clare Landi, Judith Chamberlain, Margaret Goddard,
Joyce Buzza, Sandra Richardson, Joyce Limon, Janet Mann, Yvonne Rawlinson,
Teresa Gogay, Ann Banks, Barbara Wiltshire, Joan Pavey, Jenny Cooper, Mary
Wilmot, Glennis Garnett, Audrey Kidd, Susan Grimes, Barbara Hooper, Joyce
Sledmore, Mrs Pickering, Janet Oakey, Carol Bayless, Betty Lumley

British Library Cataloging in Publication Data
A record of this book is available from the British Library

ISBN 978-1-906007-29-4
Copyright © Rowan Yarns 2007
Printed in Singapore

THE ROWAN STORY BOOK OF
Little Knits

A charming story & collection of 25 hand knit
designs for children aged 3-10 years

MARIE WALLIN

ROWAN

Molly

Elliot

Dorothy

Albert

Emily

Harriet

Monkey

Daisy

Hector

Lucy

Grumpy Ted

Toby

Scruffy Dog

CONTENTS

Charlie

Barney

Rosie

Little Cat

NCE UPON A TIME, DEEP IN THE OXFORDSHIRE COUNTRYSIDE LIVED A DELIGHTFUL LADY CALLED EMILY. EMILY LIVED IN A BEAUTIFUL OLD FARMHOUSE WHICH SHE SHARED WITH HER TWO FAITHFUL DOGS, HECTOR AND BARNEY AND SEVERAL CATS... SO MANY IT'S HARD TO REMEMBER THEIR NAMES. THIS WAS A SPECIAL PLACE, THERE WAS A HUGE GARDEN TO RUN AROUND AND PLAY IN, A TREE HOUSE TO EXPLORE, BUT BEST OF ALL WERE THE APPLES, MASSES AND MASSES OF APPLES...

TAKING INSPIRATION FROM NINE CHILDREN, A PLETHORA OF APPLES AND TWO NAUGHTY DOGS, 'LITTLE KNITS' IS A CHARMING STORY AND COLLECTION OF 25 HAND KNIT DESIGNS FOR GIRLS & BOYS, AGED THREE TO TEN YEARS BROUGHT TO YOU BY ROWAN.

BE INSPIRED, BE ENCHANTED...

Apples for Tea

 T WAS A CHILLY BUT SUNNY AUTUMNAL DAY IN OCTOBER WHEN DOROTHY, LUCY AND THEIR FRIENDS ARRIVED AT EMILY'S HOUSE.

Dorothy was desperate to go and explore from the first moment she saw the house appear through the early morning mist. She whispered excitedly in Lucy's ear. "Let's leave the others and sneak outside and play, Emily said we could pick some apples for tea."

So whilst no one was looking, Dorothy and Lucy crept quietly on tip toes out of the door. They ran expectantly into the garden, and immediately saw a swing in the biggest apple tree they had ever seen. Dorothy and Lucy had great fun taking turns on the swing and playing with an old umbrella they had discovered behind a rose bush.

It seemed a long time had passed when they suddenly remembered the apples for tea. So they quickly ran into the orchard to gather as many apples as they could carry…

DOROTHY AND LUCY HAD GREAT FUN TAKING
TURNS PLAYING ON THE SWING.

Gosling (left) & Starling (right)

"Let's pick as many apples as we can,"
said Dorothy to Lucy.

CHAPTER TWO

The Tree House

HE NEXT MORNING TOBY DECIDED TO EXPLORE THE TREE HOUSE. TOBY WAS A MISCHIEVOUS LITTLE BOY AND EASILY PERSUADED LUCY TO TAKE SOME APPLES TO THE TREE HOUSE SO THEY COULD HAVE A NICE PICNIC.

Lucy merrily went off with her basket to collect some apples. When she arrived at the tree house there was no sign of Toby, so she climbed up the ladder and waited.

Luckily, Lucy had her teddy for company and her knitting to keep her busy. A long time had passed before Lucy began to wonder what had happened to Toby. "Where can he be?" she said to herself, "I'm getting hungry."

Eventually Toby climbed into the tree house. After he had got his breath back he explained what had happened. "Sorry Lucy," he said. "The others wanted me to play with them in the stable yard, and it was really difficult to sneak away. Anyway I'm here now, shall we eat the apples, I'm starving!"

Eagerly, Lucy and Toby began to tuck into the apples that Lucy had carefully collected earlier. The apples were deliciously sweet and juicy and it didn't take them long to polish them all off. They then spent the rest of the afternoon happily playing 'I Spy'.

Whilst Lucy and Toby were playing, Lucy's teddy was getting rather hungry and had become quite grumpy. "Those greedy children have eaten all the apples, even the one I was saving for my lunch," he grumbled…

LUCY CLIMBED THE LADDER TO THE TREE HOUSE
SO SHE COULD WAIT FOR TOBY.

Peregrine

Pigeon (left) & Wren (right)

"LET'S EAT THE APPLES NOW," SAID TOBY
"I'M STARVING!"

"THOSE GREEDY CHILDREN HAVE EATEN ALL THE APPLES,"
GRUMBLED GRUMPY TED.

Osprey

CHAPTER THREE

The Dog with Many Friends

EANWHILE IN THE STABLE YARD, ELLIOT AND HARRIET WERE HAVING GREAT FUN PLAYING AT THE WENDY HOUSE WITH HECTOR.

Hector was rather a clever dog. It didn't take him long to work out that if he pinched the basket of apples laying by the side of the Wendy house, he could make Elliot and Harriet chase him around the garden, which was enormous fun for him!

Whilst Elliot, Harriet and Hector were playing, Rosie, Charlie and Molly arrived back from riding lessons with Emily. Charlie immediately disappeared into one of the stables, much to Rosie's annoyance. Rosie shouted to Charlie, "Charlie what are you doing, why don't you come out and play?" "I'll be out in a second Rosie, wait and see what I have found," replied Charlie.

Charlie soon emerged from the stable holding a rather old and battered trombone. "I bet you can't play that thing," Rosie said laughing. "Let's see," said Charlie and began to play the trombone. The sound that greeted Rosie was so awful she had to cover her ears!

Luckily out of earshot, Molly was busy putting her riding tack away. The saddle was so heavy that she had to sit down and rest a while. It was then that she noticed Elliot and Harriet trying to catch Hector... it was the funniest thing she had seen all day!

Jay (left) & Skylark (right)

Brambling

ROSIE ARRIVED BACK FROM RIDING LESSONS.

THE SOUND THAT GREETED ROSIE WAS SO AWFUL
SHE HAD TO COVER HER EARS!

Robin

Serin

MOLLY KEPT HERSELF BUSY BY PUTTING AWAY
HER RIDING TACK.

Sparrow

The Allotment

MILY COULD SEE FROM THE KITCHEN WINDOW THAT THE CHILDREN WERE HAVING FUN IN THE STABLE YARD, SO SHE DECIDED TO LET THEM PLAY A LITTLE LONGER.

After a while she went outside to call them to come indoors and change from their riding clothes.

She then said to Rosie, Charlie and Molly, "I would really like you to go into the allotment and dig up some vegetables for supper. Run along quickly as I fear it may start raining soon."

Rosie, Charlie and Molly cheerily skipped to the allotment. Rosie rather liked gardening, but much preferred flowers to vegetables, so she said to Charlie, "I'm going to pot up some pansies for Emily, you go and do the digging." "That's not fair," Charlie said sulkily as he walked into the vegetable patch.

Molly felt quite sorry for Charlie, so she decided to help him. Unfortunately for Molly, the garden spade was far too

big and heavy for her, so she sat down feeling very sad. "Don't be sad Molly," said Charlie. "I can dig up the vegetables; you go and water those onions over there, they look thirsty to me." Molly's mood lightened as she began to water the onions with a lovely green watering can she had found in the green house.

Charlie secretly enjoyed digging up the vegetables. He dug up some delicious looking potatoes and picked some plump lettuces for tea. "Emily should be really pleased with these," he said to himself.

Meanwhile back at the house, Dorothy decided she wanted to help Emily by watering the potted plants. She had almost finished when she noticed it had started to go dark. "I think it's going to rain," she said to herself. She held out her hands and very soon she felt the first drops of rain. "Everyone indoors," she shouted. "It's raining!"

Nightingale

Magpie

CHARLIE SECRETLY ENJOYED DIGGING UP THE VEGETABLES.

Curlew

"Eveyone indoors," Dorothy shouted.

"It's raining!"

Pipit (left) & Lapwing (right)

The Cake and the Missing Apples

THE CHILDREN STARTLED EMILY BY BURSTING THROUGH THE KITCHEN DOOR. "EMILY, EMILY, IT'S RAINING OUTSIDE.

We've finished all our chores, can we please come inside and play?" Emily smiled at them and kindly said "Of course children and thank you for helping me. As a special treat would you like to help me bake a cake for supper?" "Oh yes please!" Rosie quickly shouted. Just at that moment Lucy's friend Daisy walked into the kitchen. "Can I help too Emily?" pleaded Daisy.

Emily showed Rosie and Daisy how to bake a cake whilst Charlie and Molly went off to wash their hands.

It was a long time before the cake was finally finished. "It's the most beautiful cake I have ever seen," said Rosie excitedly. "Thank you," said Emily and then asked the girls to watch the cake while she went off to find the basket of apples that Hector had pinched earlier.

"Daisy, you stay here and guard the cake while I go and find Dorothy," said Rosie. A few moments had passed when Hector came running into the kitchen. He immediately skidded to an abrupt halt as he saw the cake on the table. Hector thought that

Linnet

if he went and sat next to Daisy and looked hard enough at the cake, somehow he could will it into his mouth! Unfortunately for Hector, Daisy was not letting the cake out her sight.

In the meantime Rosie found Dorothy cleaning the shoes in the parlour. "Why are you cleaning those Dorothy?" asked Rosie looking puzzled. "Well I was just about to come into the kitchen, when I saw all these muddy shoes on the floor and I thought it would help Emily if I cleaned them for her," said Dorothy. "That's really thoughtful of you. Have you seen the basket of apples that was outside earlier, Emily is looking for it?" "No Rosie, I haven't seen the apples," replied Dorothy untruthfully. Disappointedly Rosie left to see if Elliot and Harriet had seen them.

Dorothy checked to see if anyone was looking and when she thought it was safe, she opened the cupboard door and put the missing basket of apples on the table. "I know I shouldn't have taken the apples, but I found them in the stable yard. I didn't know they were Emily's," she said to herself sadly. "I just love apples so much!" Thankfully, Dorothy decided to go and find Emily and tell her she had found the apples. Emily was pleased that Dorothy had admitted to taking the apples and went with her to fetch them back. When they walked into the parlour Dorothy shouted "Oh no, the apples are gone, some one else has taken them!" Dorothy became very upset as she thought she had let Emily down. Emily put her arm around Dorothy and said "Don't worry, we will find them. I think I know who may have them." Emily quickly opened the pantry door, and to Dorothy's surprise there sat Charlie's scruffy dog in the basket of apples looking rather startled. "I knew it would be you," said Emily laughing. "I saw you sneaking around earlier!"

Swift

"DOROTHY HAVE YOU SEEN THE BASKET OF APPLES?"
SAID ROSIE.

Dove

A startled Scruffy Dog was caught red-handed!

CHAPTER SIX

The Story Teller

ROSIE POPPED HER HEAD AROUND THE LIBRARY DOOR TO SEE IF HARRIET AND ELLIOT WERE THERE.

There was no sign of them, but what she did see was Toby half way up the book case ladder. "Toby, be careful. What are you doing up there?" she asked. "I'm trying to find a book as Albert has promised to read me a story," he replied.

Albert was a very special little dog; he was very clever and exceptionally fond of books. Albert was also extremely short sighted. He was hardly ever seen outside the house, and so consequently he ate, slept and of course read in the library!

Ignoring Rosie, Toby continued his search for a good book. Whilst he was up the ladder he noticed a dusty toy monkey sat on the top shelf. "He looks quite old," thought Toby to himself. "He must belong to Emily, I'm sure she won't mind if I play with him." So he took the monkey from the shelf and headed back down the ladder.

Raven

At that moment Harriet ran into the room. "What have you got there, Toby?" she asked looking puzzled. "It's an old monkey I found on the book case," replied Toby. "Can I have a look at him please?" asked Harriet with a mischievous glint in her eyes. Before Toby could reply, Harriet snatched the monkey out of Toby's hand. "Give him back, Harriet!" shouted Toby, who was very annoyed now. "Get him if you can!" teased Harriet as she jumped up and down on the sofa with the monkey on her shoulder, just out of reach of Toby!

Both children suddenly stopped as they heard a "Huh hmm, huh hmm" coming from the door way. At that moment Albert slowly walked into the library and said in a croaky voice, "What is all this commotion? A library should be a place of peace and quiet, not of riotous behaviour!" "Sorry Albert," said Toby and Harriet sheepishly. "Will you please read us a story?" Happy that the children had asked him to read them a story, he merrily said "Of course, as long as you remain silent!"

Just then Molly said "I've found a good book." Toby and Harriet turned around in surprise. They hadn't noticed Molly in the corner as she had been so quiet. "Good," said Albert. "Are you all sitting comfortably? I shall begin."

"Once upon a time…"

"GIVE HIM BACK, HARRIET!" SHOUTED TOBY.

Kite

Quail

Duckling

CHAPTER SEVEN

A Fond Farewell

HE TIME HAD ARRIVED FOR THE CHILDREN TO LEAVE EMILY'S HOUSE. DOROTHY, LUCY AND ELLIOT WERE THE FIRST TO LEAVE.

They each took turns to give Emily a big hug and to cuddle Hector and Barney. "Thank you Emily for such a super time," they said as they happily skipped towards their father's waiting car.

Toby, Rosie, Charlie and of course Scruffy Dog were the next to leave. Scruffy Dog was not at all happy as they walked up the garden path. "It's a shame to leave all those apples," he whispered in Charlie's ear. "Don't worry," Charlie said, "I've got a big juicy apple for you in my bag!" Scruffy Dog immediately cheered up.

As Emily was saying goodbye to Toby, Rosie and Charlie, Daisy came out of the house with her suitcase. Her case was quite heavy so she put it down and said goodbye to the little ginger cat that came to sit by her feet. "Goodbye Little Cat," she said as she patted the cat on the head. "I'm going to miss being here; I've really enjoyed it, especially making the cake with Emily." Little Cat just looked up at her and meowed "Goodbye!"

Finally, it was Molly's turn to leave. Although Molly had been very quiet most of the time, she was very sad to leave Emily's house. "Emily, can I please stay here with you?" she said tearfully and clutching Grumpy Ted. Emily smiled at Molly and said "You can stay here if you like Molly, but I think your mother would be upset if you did!" Molly suddenly thought of her mother at home and quickly jumped up and kissed Emily on the cheek and said

"Thank you for everything, Emily. I must leave now as mummy will miss me." As Molly ran up the garden path she turned to wave a final goodbye to Emily. Emily fondly waved back and then went into the house leaving Barney to close the door. Barney looked up the garden path to see Molly disappear through the gate. "Bye, bye Molly!" he barked. "Come back again soon." Unfortunately for Barney, Molly did not hear him, so he turned and sadly closed the door.

Grumpy Ted was quite relieved to get into the car, as Molly had been holding him very tightly! Ted was mostly grumpy by nature and although he grumbled a lot whilst he was at Emily's house, he did secretly enjoy being there! Whilst Molly was not looking, he climbed up from the seat to see the house pulling away in the distance, as the car quickly sped away. "See you next year Emily," he said quietly to himself. He then sat back down and fell into a deep, deep sleep. He began to dream …

Peacock

GRUMPY TED WAS RELIEVED TO GET INTO THE CAR AS
MOLLY HAD BEEN HOLDING HIM VERY TIGHTLY!

"COME BACK AGAIN SOON," BARKED BARNEY.

The End

Little Knits

THE PATTERNS

Gosling

Sarah Hatton

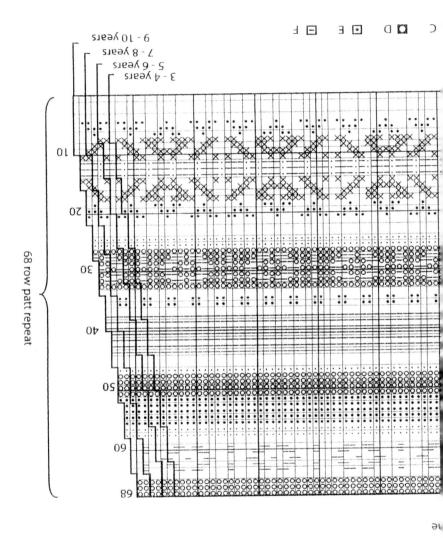

C ☐ D ☒ E ☐ F

9 - 10 years
7 - 8 years
5 - 6 years
3 - 4 years

68 row patt repeat

10
20
30
40
50
60
68

VAN

The Rowan St

P

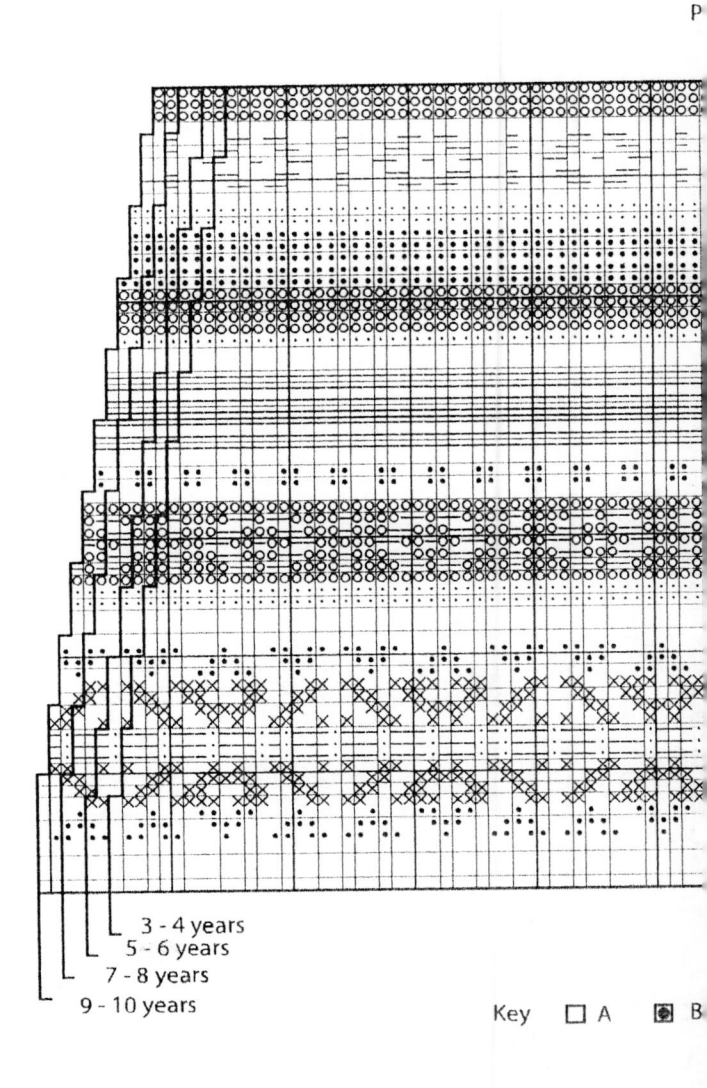

3 - 4 years
5 - 6 years
7 - 8 years
9 - 10 years

Key   ☐ A   ◉ B

SIZE

3/4	5/6	7/8	9/10	yrs

To fit chest

55–57	59–61	63–67	69–73	cm

YARN

Rowan 4 ply Cotton
Yarn A (Cream 153)

6	7	7	8	x 50g

Yarn B (Mandarine 142)

1	1	1	1	x 50g

Yarn C (Ardour 130)

1	1	1	1	x 50g

Yarn D (Aegean 129)

1	1	1	1	x 50g

NEEDLES

1 pair 3mm (no 11) (USA 3) needles

TENSION

29 sts and 39 rows to 10cm over st st on 3mm (USA 3)
needles

BACK

Using 3mm (USA 3) needles and yarn A, cast on
113 [119, 125, 131] sts.

Row 1 – * K2, P1, rep from * to last 2 sts, K2.
Row 2 – P2, * K1, P2, rep from * to end.
These 2 rows form 2x1 rib.
Work 4 rows more in rib.
Working in st st and using fairisle technique described
on information page, work 34 rows following chart A
and shaping sides by dec 1 st at each end of 17th [21st,
25th, 29th] and every foll 16th [0, 0, 0] of these rows.
109 [117, 123, 129] sts.
Cont in yarn A only dec 1 st at each end of 15th [3rd,
7th, 11th] and every foll 16th row to
99 [105, 111, 117] sts.
Work 5 rows more, ending with RS facing for next row.
Following chart B, work first 12 rows. (Back should
meas 35 [36, 37, 38]cm)
Shape armholes
Working rows 13-34 of chart as set, then repeating the
34 row patt throughout cast off
5 [4, 4, 3] sts at beg of next 2 rows. 89 [97, 103, 111] sts.
Dec 1 st at each end of next 5 rows, then foll 2 alt
rows, then foll 4th row.
73 [81, 87, 95] sts. **
Cont straight until armhole meas 18.5 [19.5,
20.5, 21.5]cm, ending with RS facing for next row.
Shape shoulders
Cast off 5 [6, 6, 7] sts at beg of next 2 rows.
63 [69, 75, 81] sts.

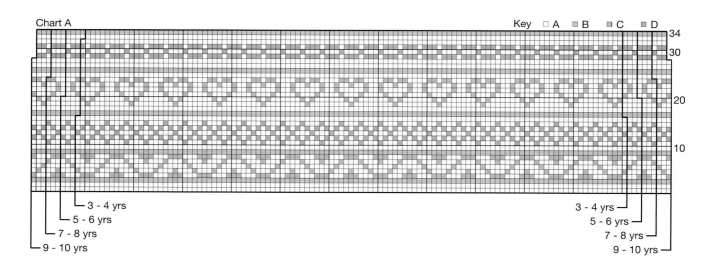

Chart A

Key □ A ▨ B ▨ C ▨ D

34
30

20

10

3 - 4 yrs
5 - 6 yrs
7 - 8 yrs
9 - 10 yrs

3 - 4 yrs
5 - 6 yrs
7 - 8 yrs
9 - 10 yrs

Next row – Cast off 5 [6, 7, 8] sts, patt until there are
9 [10, 11, 12] sts on right hand needle, turn and work
this side first.
Next row – Cast off 4 sts, patt to end.
Cast off rem 5 [6, 7, 8] sts.
With RS facing, cast off centre 35 [37, 39, 41] sts, patt
to end.
Complete to match first side reversing shapings.

FRONT

Work as given for back to **.
Cont straight until 34 [34, 34, 36] rows less have been
worked than Back to shoulder shaping.

Divide for neck

Next row – Patt 32 [36, 39, 43], turn and work this
side first.
Work 30 rows more, ending with WS facing for next row.

Shape neck

Next row – (WS) Cast off 12 [13, 14, 13] sts, patt to
end. 20 [23, 25, 30] sts.
Dec 1 st at neck edge in next 2 [2, 2, 4] rows.
18 [21, 23, 26] sts.

Shape shoulder

Cast off 5 [6, 6, 7] sts at beg of next and 5 [6, 7, 8] sts
at beg of foll alt row **at same time** dec 1 st at neck

edge in every row.
Work 1 row more.
Cast off rem 5 [6, 7, 8] sts.
With RS facing, rejoin yarn to rem sts, cast off centre
9 sts, patt to end.
Complete to match first side reversing shapings and
working 1 row less before neck shaping.

SLEEVES (Both alike)

Using 3mm (USA 3) needles and yarn A, cast on
98 [101, 101, 104] sts.
Beg with row 1, work 6 rows in 2x1 rib as given for
Back, inc 1 [0, 2, 1] sts in last of these rows.
99 [101, 103, 105] sts.
Beg with a K row work 2 rows in st st.
Work 10 rows foll chart C.
Cont in yarn A only shaping sides by dec 1 st at each
end of 41st row. 97 [99, 101, 103] sts.
Cont straight until sleeve meas 16 [20, 24, 28]cm,
ending with RS facing for next row

Shape top

Cast off 5 [4, 4, 3] sts at beg of next 2 rows.
87 [91, 93, 97] sts.
Dec 1 st at each end of next 10 rows. 67 [71, 73, 77] sts.
Cast off 11 [13, 14, 16] sts at beg of next 2 rows. 45 sts.

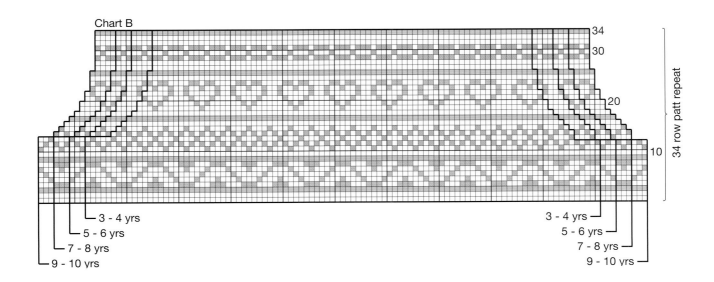

Chart B
34 row patt repeat

3 - 4 yrs
5 - 6 yrs
7 - 8 yrs
9 - 10 yrs

Chart C

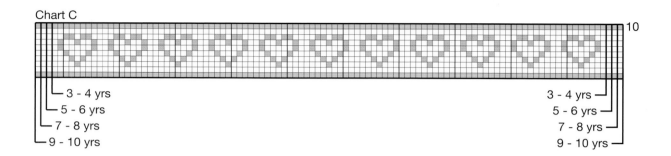

└ 3 - 4 yrs
└ 5 - 6 yrs
└ 7 - 8 yrs
└ 9 - 10 yrs

3 - 4 yrs ┘
5 - 6 yrs ┘
7 - 8 yrs ┘
9 - 10 yrs ┘

Cast off 14 sts at beg of next 2 rows.
Cast off rem 17 sts.

MAKING UP
Front neck slit edgings (both alike)
With RS facing using 3mm (USA 3) needles and yarn A,
pick up and knit 26sts evenly along selvedge of front
neck slit.
Beg with row 2 of 2x1 rib as given for Back work 5 rows.
Cast off.
Sew ends to cast off edge at bottom of slit.
Join shoulder seams.
Neck edging
With RS facing using 3mm (USA 3) needles and yarn A,
pick up and knit 4 sts from front neck slit edging, 25
[25, 25, 27] sts up right side of neck, 40 [43, 46, 48] sts
from back neck, 25 [25, 25, 27] sts down left side of
neck and 4 sts from front neck slit edging.
98 [101, 104, 110] sts.
Beg with row 2 of 2x1 rib as given for Back, work 5 rows
in rib. Cast off.
Join side and sleeve seams. Insert sleeves.
Belt
Using 3mm (USA 3) needles and yarn A, cast on 11 sts.
Row 1 – (RS) (K2, P1) 3 times, K2.

Row 2 – K1, P1, K1, (P2, K1) twice, P1 K1.
These 2 rows form rib.
Cont in rib until belt meas 110cm, ending with RS
facing for next row.
Cast off.

16 [20: 24: 28] cm
(6 1/2 [8: 9 1/2: 11] in)

55 [57: 59: 61] cm
(21 1/2 [22 1/2: 23: 24] in)

34.5 [36.5: 38.5: 40.5] cm
(13 1/2 [14 1/2: 15: 16] in)

Starling
Marie Wallin

Starling (right)

SIZE

	3/4	5/6	7/8	9/10	yrs

To fit chest

55–57	59–61	63–67	69–73	cm

YARN

Rowan Cotton Glace (Ecru 725)

6	7	7	8	x 50g

NEEDLES

1 x 3.00mm (no 11) (USA C2) crochet hook

TENSION

19 sts and 11 rows to 10cm over treble fabric on 3.00mm (USA C2) crochet hook

CROCHET ABBREVIATIONS

ch = chain; ss = slip stitch; dc = double crochet; tr = treble; tog = together; ch sp = chain space.

SPECIAL ABBREVIATIONS

dtr2tog = work dtr into next st until 1 loop of each remains on hook, yo and through all loops on hook.
qtr = work as dtr but wrapping yarn 4 times over hook.

BACK

Using 3.00mm (USA C2) hook make 83 [83, 92, 92] chain.
Row 1 – (RS) 1tr into 8th ch from hook, * 2ch, miss 2ch, 1tr into next ch, rep from * to end, turn.
Row 2 – 1ch, 1dc into 1st tr, * 9ch, miss 1 tr, (1dc, 4ch, dtr2tog) into next tr, miss 1 tr, (dtr2tog, 4ch, 1dc) into next tr, rep from * to last 2ch sps, 9ch, miss 1tr, 1dc into 3rd ch, turn.
Row 3 – 10ch, 1dc into 1st 9ch sp, * 4ch, (dtr2tog, 4ch, 1ss, 4ch, dtr2tog) into top of next dtr2tog, 4ch, 1dc into next 9ch sp, rep from * to end, 4ch, 1qtr into last dc, turn.
Row 4 – 1ch, 1dc into 1st qtr, * 5ch, 1dc into top of next dtr2tog, rep from * to end, working last dc into 6th of 10ch at beg of previous row, turn.
Row 5 – 5ch, 1tr into next ch sp, 2ch, 1tr into next dc, * 2ch, 1tr into next 5ch sp, 2ch, 1tr into next dc, rep from * to end, turn.

Rep rows 2 – 5 once more.
Next row – 1ch, * 2dc into next 2ch sp, 1dc into next tr, rep from * to last ch sp, 2dc into 2ch sp, turn.
Next row – 1ch, 1dc into each dc to end **at same time** dec 9 [5, 8, 4] sts evenly across this row by dc2tog. 74 [78, 84, 88] sts.
Mesh
Row 1 – (RS) 3ch, miss 1dc, 1tr into next dc, * 1ch, miss 1dc, 1tr into next dc, rep from * to end, turn.
Row 2 – 3ch, miss 1tr into next tr, * 1ch, 1tr into next tr, rep from * to end, ending last tr into 2nd ch of 3ch from previous row, turn.
Rep row 2 twice more.
Next row – (RS) 3ch, * 1tr into ch sp, 1tr into next tr, rep from * to end, turn.
Next row – 3ch, * 1tr into each tr to end, turn.
Rep last row dec 1 st at each end of next and 4 foll 3rd rows. 64 [68, 74, 78] sts.
Work 3 [5, 7, 9] rows straight.
Inc 1 st at each end of next and 2 foll 4th rows. 70 [74, 80, 84] sts.
Cont straight until back meas 41 [42, 43, 44]cm, ending with RS facing for next row.
Shape armholes
Next row – Ss across 1st 3tr of previous row, 2ch, 1tr into each tr to last 3trs of previous row, turn. 64 [68, 74, 78] sts.
Next row – Tr2tog, 2ch, 1tr into each tr to last 2tr of previous row, Tr2tog, turn. 62 [66, 72, 76] sts.
Next row – 2ch, 1tr into each tr to end, turn.
Rep last row until armhole meas 15.5 [16.5, 17.5, 18.5]cm, ending with RS facing for next row.
Fasten off.

FRONT

Work as given for Back until 7 [7, 7, 9]rows less have been worked than on Back.
Shape neck
Work across 1st 18 [19, 20, 21] tr, turn and work this side first.
Next row – Ss across first 4trs, tr to end. 14 [15, 16, 17] sts.
Dec 1 st at neck edge in next 3 rows. 11 [12, 13, 14] sts.
Cont straight until front matches Back. Fasten off.
Rejoin yarn, work to match first side.

MAKING UP

Hem edging (Back and front like)

With RS facing rejoin yarn to hem, 1dc into 1st tr, *
2dc into 2ch sp, 1dc into next tr, rep from * to last 3ch
sp, 2dc into 3ch sp, turn.

Next row – 1ch, 1dc into each dc to end, turn.

Row 1 – (RS) 5ch, miss 1st 3dc, 1dc into next dc, work
3 picots (3ch, ss into 1st ch) 3 times, 1dc into next dc, *
5ch, mis 4dc, 1dc into next dc, work 3 picots, 1dc into
next dc, rep from * to last 3dc, 2ch, 1tr into last dc, turn.

Row 2 – 1ch, 1dc into 1st tr, * 8ch, 1dc into 5ch sp, rep
from * to end, working last dc into 3rd of 5ch at beg of
previous row, turn.

Row 3 – 1ch, 1dc into 1st dc, * 11dc, into next 3ch sp,
1dc into next dc, rep from * to end. Fasten off. Join
side and shoulder seams.

Armhole and neck edging (alike)

Work dcs evenly all around edge.

Next row – * miss 1dc, 4dc into next dc, rep from * to
end, ss to 2ch at beg of round. Fasten off.

59 [61:63:65] cm
(23 [24:25:26] in)

37 [39:42:44.5] cm
(14 1/2 [15 1/2:16 1/2:17 1/2] in)

Peregrine
Marie Wallin

SIZE

	3/4	5/6	7/8	9/10	yrs

To fit chest

	55–57	59–61	63–67	69–73	cm

YARN

Rowan Calmer
Yarn A (Plum 493)

	2	3	3	3	x 50g

Yarn B (Garnet 492)

	1	1	2	2	x 50g

Yarn C (Coffee Bean 481)

	1	1	2	2	x 50g

Yarn D (Cork 491)

	1	1	2	2	x 50g

Yarn E (Slosh 479)

	1	1	1	1	x 50g

Yarn F (Calm 461)

	1	1	2	2	x 50g

NEEDLES

1 pair 4mm (no 8) (USA 6) needles
1 pair 4½mm (no 7) (USA 7) needles
1 x 3.50mm (no 9) (USA E4) crochet hook

TENSION

23 sts and 30 rows to 10cm over patt on 4½mm
(USA 7) needles
20sts and 23 rows to 10cm over crochet using 3.50mm
(USA E4) crochet hook

BODICE STRIPE SEQUENCE

Row 1 – Yarn A
Row 2 – Yarn D
Row 3 – Yarn B
Row 4 – Yarn C

BACK

Using 4mm (USA 6) needles and yarn A, cast on
109 [113, 117, 121] sts.
Work 2 rows in g st.
Change to 4½mm (USA 7) needles

Beg with a K row, working in st st and using fairisle
technique described on information page, rep 68 rows
of chart shaping sides by dec 1 st at each end of
9th [9th, 11th, 11th] and every foll 6th row to 79 [83,
87, 91] sts.
Cont straight until back meas 38.5 [39.5, 40.5, 41.5]cm,
ending with RS facing for next row. Cast off.
Bodice
With RS facing using 3.50 mm (USA E4) crochet hook
and yarn A, 1ch, work 69 [73, 77, 81] dcs evenly across
entire row. Working first and last 9 dcs in yarn A and
centre 51 [55, 59, 63] dcs as Bodice stripe sequence beg
with Row 2, work 3 rows. **
Shape armholes
Next row – (RS) using yarn A, ss across first 5dcs, 1ch,
1dc into each of next 4 dcs, next 51 [55, 59, 63] dcs
worked in Bodice stripe sequence, next 4dcs in yarn A,
turn.
Cont as set until armhole meas 14.5 [15.5, 16.5, 17.5]cm,
ending with RS facing for next row.
Shape back neck
Using yarn A, 1ch, 1dc into next 4 dcs, keeping Bodice
stripe sequence, 1dc into each of next 10 [12, 14, 16] dcs,
turn.
Next row – 1ch, 1dc into each of next 10 [12, 14, 16] dcs
in patt, 1dc into each of next 4 dcs in yarn A. Fasten off.
Work second side to match.

FRONT

Work as given for back to **.
Shape armholes
Next row – (RS) Using yarn A ss across first 5 dcs, 1ch,
1dc into each of next 4 dcs, next 25 [27, 29, 31] dcs
worked in Bodice stripe sequence, turn.
Next row – Keeping 4dcs at armhole edge in yarn A
throughout and rest as Bodice stripe sequence, dc2tog,
at beg of next and every foll alt row to 14 [16, 18, 20] sts.
Cont straight until front matches Back to fasten off.
Fasten off.
Work second side to match first.

MAKING UP

Join side and shoulder seams.

Neckband

Using 3.50mm (USA E4) crochet hook and yarn A, beg at right side neck:-

Round 1 – 1ch, 1dc evenly around entire neck, dc2tog at centre of V, ss to first dc at end of round. Work 1 more round. Fasten off.

Hem fringing

Using 12 lengths of yarn A, 12cm long and crochet

hook pull through hem of dress and thread ends through.

Make fringes at 4cm intervals all around hem using yarns A, C and D.

Trim ends to neaten.

Stitched detail

Using yarns C and D double, work stitching using diagram as a guide.

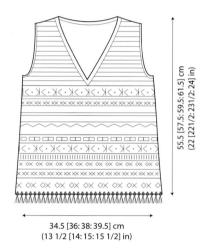

55.5 [57.5: 59.5: 61.5] cm
(22 [22 1/2: 23 1/2: 24] in)

34.5 [36: 38: 39.5] cm
(13 1/2 [14: 15: 15 1/2] in)

Pigeon
Marie Wallin

Pigeon (left)

SIZE

3/4	5/6	7/8	9/10	yrs

To fit chest

55–57	59–61	63–67	69–73	cm

YARN

Rowan Denim
Yarn A (Tennessee 231)

7	8	9	10	x 50g

Yarn B (Nashville 225)

2	2	2	2	x 50g

NEEDLES

1 pair 3¾mm (no 9) (USA 5) needles

TENSION

20 sts and 28 rows to 10cm over st st on 3¾mm
(USA 5) needles
(21 sts and 32 rows after finishing)

STRIPE SEQUENCE

Back, Front and Hood
Rows 1 to 12 – Yarn A
Rows 13 and 14 – Yarn B
These 14 rows are repeated
Sleeve
Rows 1 and 2 – Yarn A
Rows 3 and 4 – Yarn B
Rows 5 to 14 – Yarn A
These 14 rows are repeated

BACK

Using 3¾mm (USA 5) needles and yarn A cast on
70 [74, 78, 82] sts.
Purl 4 rows. **
Beg with a K row, cont in st st working in stripe
sequence as set for Back, Front and Hood until back
meas 25.5 [27, 27.5, 29]cm, ending with RS facing for
next row.
Shape armholes
Cast off 5 sts at beg of next 2 rows. 60 [64, 68, 72] sts.
Dec 1 st at each end of next 3 rows, then foll 2 alt
rows. 50 [54, 58, 62] sts.
Cont straight until armhole meas 17.5 [18.5,
19.5, 20.5]cm, ending with RS facing for next row.

Shape shoulders
Cast off 3 [3, 4, 4] sts at beg of next 2 rows.
44 [48, 50, 54] sts.
Cast off 4 sts at beg of next 2 rows.
Cast off rem 36 [40, 42, 46] sts.

FRONT

Work as given for Back to **.
Beg with a K row, cont in st st work 36 [38, 40, 42] rows
in stripe sequence as set for Back, Front and Hood
ending with RS facing for next row.
Leave sts on a spare needle.
Pocket
With RS facing using 3¾mm (USA 5) needles and yarn
A, pick up and K centre 50 sts from 1st st st row.
Beg with a P row working in stripe sequence to match
front, work 15 [17, 19, 21] rows, ending with RS facing
for next row.
Cast off 4 sts at beg of next 2 rows. 42 sts.
Dec 1 st at each end of next 5 rows, then 2 foll alt
rows. 28 sts.
Work 9 rows straight, ending with RS facing for next
row, break yarn.
Next row – Rejoin yarn and K across first 21 [23,
25, 27] sts of front, Ktog 28 sts from pocket and next
28 sts of front, K to end. 70 [74, 78, 82] sts.
Cont straight until front matches back to armhole
shaping, ending with RS facing for next row.
Shape armholes
Cast off 5 sts at beg of next 2 rows. 60 [64, 68, 72] sts.
Dec 1 st at each end of next 3 rows, then 2 foll alt
rows. 50 [54, 58, 62] sts.
Cont straight until 12 [12, 12, 14] rows less have been
worked than on Back to shoulder shaping.
Shape neck
Next row – K21 [23, 25, 27], turn and work this side
first.
Cast off 4 [5, 5, 6] sts at beg of next and 4 [5, 6, 7] sts
at beg of foll alt row. 13 [13, 14, 14] sts.
Dec 1 st at neck edge in next 6 rows. 7 [7, 8, 8] sts.
Cont straight until front matches back to shoulder
shaping, ending with RS facing for next row.
Shape shoulder
Next row – Cast off 3 [3, 4, 4] sts, K to end.
Work 1 row more.
Cast off rem 4 sts.

With RS rejoin yarn to rem sts, cast off centre 8 sts, K to end.
Complete to match first side reversing shapings and working 1 row more before shoulder shaping.

SLEEVES (Both alike)
Using 3¾mm (USA 5) needles and yarn A cast on 36 [38, 40, 42] sts.
Work 4 rows in g st.
Beg with a K row and working in stripe sequence as set for Sleeves work 9 rows in st st.
These 13 rows form turn back cuff.
Next row – (New RS) Beg with a K row, cont in st st and stripe sequence shaping sides by inc 1 st at each end of 11th and every foll 6th [8th, 10th, 10th] row to 42 [52, 62, 54] sts.

Sizes 3/4, 5/6 and 9/10 yrs only
Inc 1 st at each end of every foll 8th [10th, -, 12th] row to 58 [60, -, 64] sts.
All sizes
Cont straight until sleeve meas 35 [39.5, 44, 48.5]cm excluding turn back cuff, ending with RS facing for next row.

Shape top
Cast off 5 sts at beg of next 2 rows. 48 [50, 52, 54] sts.

Dec 1 st at each end of next 6 rows.
36 [38, 40, 42] sts.
Cast off 6 [7, 8, 9] sts at beg of next 2 rows.
Cast off rem 24 sts.

MAKING UP
Join side, sleeve and shoulder seams.
Hood
Using 3¾mm (USA 5) needles and yarn A cast on 114 [118, 122, 126] sts.
Purl 4 rows.
Beg with a K row, cont in st st working stripe sequence as set for Back, Front and Hood, shaping sides by dec 1 st at each end of 15th and 2 foll 6th rows, then on foll 4th row.
106 [110, 114, 118] sts.
Work 1 row, ending with RS facing for next row.
Next row – K2tog, K49 [51, 53, 55], K2tog, turn and work this side first.
Work 3 rows straight.
Dec 1 st at each end of next and every foll alt row to 35 sts.
Work 1 row more. Cast off.
With RS facing, rejoin yarn to rem sts, K2tog, K49 [51, 53, 55], K2tog.
Complete to match first side.
Join back seam and attach hood.

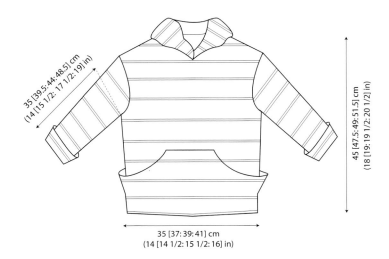

35 [39.5:44:48.5] cm
(14 [15 1/2: 17 1/2:19] in)

45 [47.5:49: 51.5] cm
(18 [19:19 1/2: 20 1/2] in)

35 [37: 39:41] cm
(14 [14 1/2: 15 1/2: 16] in)

Wren
Marie Wallin

Wren (right)

SIZE

	3/4	5/6	7/8	9/10	yrs

To fit chest

	55–57	59–61	63–67	69–73	cm

YARN

Rowan 4 ply Cotton
Yarn A (Navy 150)

	5	6	7	7	x 50g

Yarn B (Steel Blue 149)

	1	1	1	1	x 50g

Yarn C (Cream 153)

	1	1	1	1	x 50g

Yarn D (Aubergine 148)

	1	1	1	1	x 50g

NEEDLES

1 pair 3mm (no 11) (USA 3) needles
1 pair 2¾mm (no 12) (USA 2) needles
Zip fastener to fit

TENSION

29 sts and 39 rows to 10cm over st st on 3mm (USA 3) needles

STRIPE SEQUENCE

Worked in st st throughout
Rows 1 and 2 – Yarn A
Rows 3 and 4 – Yarn B
Rows 5 to 7 – Yarn A
Rows 8 and 9 – Yarn C
Rows 10 to 12 – Yarn A
Rows 13 and 14 – Yarn D
Rows 15 to 17 – Yarn A
Rows 18 and 19 – Yarn C
Rows 20 to 25 – Yarn A
Rows 26 and 27 – Yarn D
Rows 28 to 30 – Yarn A
Rows 31 and 32 – Yarn B
Rows 33 to 35 – Yarn A
Rows 36 and 37 – Yarn C

BACK

Using 2¾mm (USA 2) needles and yarn A, cast on
98 [104, 110, 114] sts.
Row 1 – (RS) * K1, P1, rep from * to end.
Row 2 - * P1, K1, rep from * to end.
These 2 rows form moss st.
Work 4 rows more in moss st.
Change to 3mm (USA 3) needles
Beg with a K row work 37 rows of stripe sequence
shaping sides by dec 1 st at each end of 27th and foll
8th of these rows. 94 [100, 106, 110] sts.
Cont in yarn A only dec 1 st at each end of 6th and foll
8th row.
90 [96, 102, 106] sts.
Work 7 rows straight.
Inc 1 st at each end of next and every foll 6th row to
102 [108, 114, 118] sts.
Cont straight until back meas 25 [26, 27, 28]cm,
ending with RS facing for next row.
Shape armholes
Cast off 5 [4, 3, 1] sts at beg of next 2 rows.
92 [100, 108, 116] sts.
Dec 1 st at each end of next 3 rows, then foll alt row.
84 [92, 100, 108] sts.
Cont straight until armhole meas 15.5 [16.5,
17.5, 18.5]cm, ending with RS facing for next row.
Shape shoulders
Cast off 6 [7, 8, 9] sts at beg of next 2 rows.
72 [78, 84, 90] sts.
Next row – Cast off 6 [7, 8, 9] sts, K until there are
11 [12, 13, 13] sts on right hand needle, turn and work
this side first.
Next row – Cast off 4 sts, P to end.
Cast off rem 7 [8, 9, 9] sts.
With RS facing rejoin yarn to rem sts, cast off centre
38 [40, 42, 46] sts, K to end.
Complete to match first side reversing shapings.

LEFT FRONT

Using 2¾mm (USA 2) needles and yarn A, cast on
46 [48, 52, 54] sts.
Work 6 rows in moss st as given for back dec 1 [0,
1, 1] st at centre of last of these rows. 45 [48, 51, 53] sts.
Change to 3mm (USA 3) needles
Beg with a K row work 37 rows of stripe sequence
shaping side by dec 1 st at side edge (beg) in 27th and
foll 8th of these rows.43 [46, 49, 51] sts.
Cont in yarn A only dec 1 st at side edge in 6th and
foll 8th row. 41 [44, 47, 49] sts.
Work 7 rows straight.
Inc 1 st at side edge in next and every foll 6th row to
47 [50, 53, 55] sts.
Cont straight until left front matches Back to armhole
shaping, ending with RS facing for next row.
Shape armhole
Next row – Cast off 5 [4, 3, 1] sts, K to end.
42 [46, 50, 54] sts.
Work 1 row more.
Dec 1 st at armhole edge of next 3 rows, then foll alt
row. 38 [42, 46, 50] sts.
Cont straight until 19 rows less have been worked
than on Back to shoulder shaping, ending with WS
facing for next row.
Shape neck
Next row – Cast off 9 [10, 11, 13] sts, P to end.
29 [32, 35, 37] sts.
Dec 1 st at neck edge in next 7 rows then 3 foll alt
rows. 19 [22, 25 27] sts.
Cont straight until left front matches Back to shoulder
shaping, ending with RS facing for next row.
Shape shoulder
Cast off 6 [7, 8, 9] sts at beg of next and foll alt row.
Work 1 row more. Cast off rem 7 [8, 9, 9] sts.

RIGHT FRONT

Work to match Left front reversing shapings, working
1 row more before armhole and shoulder shaping and
1 row less before neck shaping.

SLEEVES (Both alike)

Using 2¾mm (USA 2) needles and yarn A, cast on
52 [56, 58, 60] sts.
Work 6 rows in moss st as given for Back.
Change to 3mm (USA 3) needles
Beg with a K row work 37 rows of stripe sequence
then first 19 rows again **at same time** shaping sides
by inc 1 st at each end of 5th and every foll 4th [6th,
6th, 6th] row to 62 [74, 76, 66] sts, then in every foll
6th [-, -, 8th] row to 72 [-, -, 74] sts.
Cont in yarn A only inc 1 st at each end of 1st [3rd,
3rd, 1st] and every foll 6th [6th, 8th, 8th] row to
92 [96, 98, 100] sts.
Cont straight until sleeve meas 33 [37, 41, 45]cm,
ending with RS facing for next row.
Shape top
Cast off 5 [4, 3, 1] sts at beg of next 2 rows.
82 [88, 92, 98] sts.
Dec 1 st at each end of next 12 rows.
58 [64, 68, 74] sts.
Cast off 19 [22, 24, 27] sts at beg of next 2 rows. Cast
off rem 20 sts.

MAKING UP

Join shoulder seams.
Neckband
With RS facing using 2¾mm (USA 2) needles and yarn
A, pick up and knit 25 sts up right side of neck, 48 [50,
52, 54] sts across back neck and 25 sts down left side
of neck.
98 [100, 102, 104] sts.
Work 5 rows in moss st as given for Back. Cast off in
moss st.
Right front edging
With RS facing using 2¾mm (USA 2) needles and
yarn A, pick up and knit 111 [117, 123, 129] sts
evenly along right front edge and 5 sts from from
neck edging.
116 [122, 128, 134] sts.
Work 5 rows in moss st as given for Back.

Cast off in moss st.

Left front edging

With RS facing using 2¾mm (USA 2) needles and yarn A, pick up and knit 5 sts from neckband and 111 [117, 123, 129] sts evenly along left front edge. 116 [122, 128, 134] sts.

Work as given for Left front edging.

Join side and sleeve seams. Insert sleeves and zip.

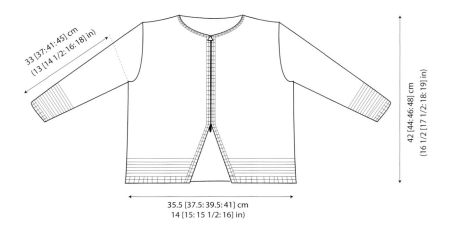

33 [37:41:45] cm
(13 [14 1/2:16:18] in)

42 [44:46:48] cm
(16 1/2 [17 1/2:18:19] in)

35.5 [37.5:39.5:41] cm
14 [15:15 1/2:16] in)

Osprey
Marie Wallin

SIZE

	3/4	5/6	7/8	9/10	yrs
To fit chest					
	55–57	59–61	63–67	69–73	cm

YARN

Rowan Denim
Yarn A (Tennessee 231)

	4	4	5	5	x 50g

Yarn B (Ecru 324)

	2	3	3	3	x 50g

Yarn C (Memphis 229)

	1	2	2	2	x 50g

Yarn D (Nashville 225)

	2	2	2	2	x 50g

NEEDLES

1 pair 4mm (no 8) (USA 6) needles
1 pair 3¾mm (no 9) (USA 5) needles
Zip fastener to fit

TENSION

20 sts and 28 rows to 10cm over st st on 4mm (USA 6) needles
(21 sts and 31 rows after finishing)

BACK

Using 4mm (USA 6) needles and yarn A, cast on 70 [74, 78, 82] sts.
Row 1 – (RS) * K2, P2, rep from * to last 2 sts, K2.
Row 2 – P2, * K2, P2, rep from * to end.
These 2 rows form 2x2 rib.
Work 6 rows more in rib.
Beg with a K row, cont in st st until back meas 28 [29.5, 30, 31.5] cm, ending with RS facing for next row.
Shape raglan
Dec 1 st at each end of next 5 rows, then every foll alt row to 28 [30, 32, 34] sts.
Work 1 row more. Cast off.

LEFT FRONT

Using 4mm (USA 6) needles and yarn A, cast on 20 [21, 22, 23] sts, then cast on 15 [16, 17, 18] sts using yarn B.
35 [37, 39, 41] sts.
Using intarsia method as described on information page for joining colours throughout and keeping each st in colour as set, proceed as follows:-
Row 1 – (RS) * K2, P2, rep from * to last 3 [1, 3, 1] sts, K3 [1, 3, 1].
Row 2 – K1, P2 [0, 2, 0], * K2, P2, rep from * to end.
These 2 rows form rib with g st edge.
Work 6 rows more in rib as set.
Row 1 – (RS) Knit.
Row 2 – K1, P to end.
These 2 rows from st st with g st edge.
Cont as set until left front meas 28 [29.5, 30, 31.5] cm, ending with RS facing for next row.
Shape raglan
Dec 1 st at armhole edge in next 5 rows, then every foll alt row to 16 [17, 18, 19] sts, ending with WS facing for next row.
Shape neck
Next row – (WS) Cast off 9 [10, 11, 12] sts, P to end. 7 sts.
Dec 1 st at raglan edge in next and foll alt row at same time dec 1 st at neck edge in every row.
Next row – Patt 2tog. Fasten off.

RIGHT FRONT

Using 4mm (USA 6) needles and yarn B, cast on 15 [16, 17, 18] sts, then cast on 20 [21, 22, 23] sts using yarn A.
35 [37, 39, 41] sts.
Row 1 – (RS) K3 [1, 3, 1], * P2, K2, rep from * to end.
Row 2 – * P2, K2, rep from * to last 3 [1, 3, 1] sts, P2 [0, 2, 0], K1.
These 2 rows form g st edge and rib.
Work 6 rows more as set.
Row 1 – (RS) Knit.
Row 2 – P to last st, K1.

These 2 rows set g st edge and st st.
Complete to match Left front reversing shapings and working 1 row more before neck shaping.

SLEEVES
Using 4mm (USA 6) needles and yarn C, cast on 7 [8, 9, 10] sts, then cast on 22 sts using yarn B and 7 [8, 9, 10] sts using yarn C.
36 [38, 40, 42] sts.
Row 1 – (RS) P1 [0, 1, 0], * K2, P2, rep from * to last 3 [2, 3, 2] sts, K2, P1 [0, 1, 0].
Row 2 – K1 [0, 1, 0], * P2, K2, rep from * to last 3 [2, 3, 2] sts, P2, K1 [0, 1, 0].
These 2 rows form rib. Work 6 rows more in rib.
Beg with a K row, cont in st st shaping sides by inc 1 st at each end of 13th and every foll 10th [12th, 12th,14th] row to 48 [52, 52, 56] sts, taking extra sts into appropriate colour.
Sizes 3/4 and 7/8 sizes only
Inc 1 st at each end of every foll 12th [-, 14th, -] row to 50 [-, 54, -] sts.

All sizes
Work 5 [5, 7, 7] rows more.
Change to yarn A only and work 6 rows straight.
Change to yarn D only and inc 1 st at each end of next row.
52 [54, 56, 58] sts.
Cont straight until sleeve meas 37.5 [42, 44, 49.5]cm, ending with RS facing for next row.
Shape raglan
Work 0 [4, 8, 12] rows dec 1 st at each end of 0 [1st, 1st, 1st] and every foll 0 [0, 4th, 4th] of these rows. 52 sts.
Dec 1 st at each end of next and every foll alt row to 20 [24, 26, 30] sts, ending with WS facing for next row.
Right sleeve only
Work 1 row.
Next row (RS) – K2tog, K6 [8, 9, 11], K2tog, turn and work this side first.
Dec 1 st at raglan edge in 2nd and 1 [2, 2, 3] foll alt

rows **at same time** dec 1 st at neck edge in next 4 [5, 6, 7] rows.
Next row – P2tog. Fasten off.
With RS facing rejoin yarn to rem sts, K8 [10, 11, 13], K2tog.
Dec 1 st at raglan edge in 2 [3, 3, 4] foll alt rows.
7 [8, 9, 10] sts.
Work 21 [23, 25, 27] rows straight in st st, ending with RS facing for next row. Cast off.
Left sleeve only
Next row – P8 [10, 11, 13], P2tog, turn and work this side first.
Dec 1 st at neck edge in next 4 [5, 6, 7] rows **at same time** dec 1 st at raglan edge in next and 2 [3, 3, 4] foll alt rows.
Next row – P2tog, fasten off.
With WS facing rejoin yarn to rem sts, P to end.
Dec 1 st at raglan edge in next and 2 [3, 3, 4] foll alt rows. 7 [8, 9, 10] sts.
Work 21 [23, 25, 27] rows straight in st st ending with RS facing for next row. Cast off.

MAKING UP
Join raglan seams.
Join cast off edges of 7 [8, 9, 10] cast off sts of shoulder extensions, then join shoulders to back cast off edge.
Neckband
Using 3¾mm (USA 5) needles and yarn B, pick up and knit 14 [14, 14, 15] sts up right side of front neck, using yarn A, pick up and knit 6 [7, 8, 8] sts from right sleeve top, 28 [30, 32, 34] sts from back neck and 6 [7, 8, 8] sts from left sleeve top, using yarn B, pick up and knit 14 [14, 14, 15] sts down left side of neck.
68 [72, 76, 80] sts.
Row 1 – (WS) K1, P2, * K2, P2, rep from * to last st, K1.
Row 2 – K1, * K2, P2, rep from * to last 3 sts, K3.
These 2 rows form rib with g st edge.
Rep last 2 rows 5 times more, then row 1 once more.
Cast off in rib.

Join side and sleeve seams.
Using photograph as a guide work the contrast

stitching across all vertical colour joints.
Wash garment. Sew in zip fastener.

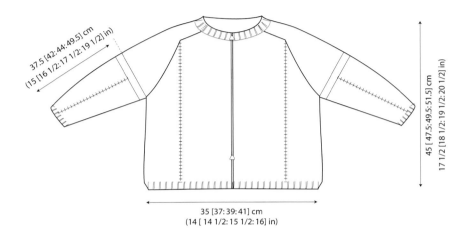

37.5 [42:44:49.5] cm
(15 [16 1/2:17 1/2:19 1/2] in)

45 [47.5:49.5:51.5] cm
17 1/2 [18 1/2:19 1/2:20 1/2] in)

35 [37:39:41] cm
(14 [14 1/2:15 1/2:16] in)

Skylark

Marie Wallin

SIZE

	3/4	5/6	7/8	9/10	yrs

To fit chest

	55–57	59–61	63–67	69–73	cm

YARN

Rowan Calmer

Yarn A (Drift 460)

	1	2	2	2	x 50g

Yarn B (Vintage 490)

	1	1	1	2	x 50g

Yarn C (Slosh 479)

	1	1	1	1	x 50g

Yarn D (Calmer 463)

	4	5	5	6	x 50g

EMBROIDERY

Rowan Calmer – oddments

Yarn E (Delight 489)

Yarn F (Sugar 488)

NEEDLES

1 pair 5mm (no 6) (USA 8) needles

1 pair 4½mm (no 7) (USA 7) needles

1 x 5.00mm (no 6) (USA H8) crochet hook

1 button

TENSION

21 sts and 30 rows to 10cm over st st on 5mm (USA 8) needles

CROCHET ABBREVIATIONS

ch = chain.

STRIPE SEQUENCE

Row 1- P using yarn A

Row 2 – K using yarn A

Row 3- K using yarn B

Row 4 – P using yarn B

Row 5 – K using Yarn A

Row 6 – P using yarn A

Rep rows 3 to 6, 8 times more

Row 39 – K using yarn C

Row 40 – P using yarn C

Rows 41 and 42 – As rows 39 and 40

BACK

Using 5mm (USA 8) needles and yarn A, cast on 72 [76, 80, 84] sts.

Work 42 rows of stripe sequence as set.

Using yarn D only, beg with a K row cont in st st shaping sides by dec 1 st at each end of next and 2 foll 8th rows. 66 [70, 74, 78] sts. **

Work 13 [13, 15, 17] rows straight.

Inc 1 st at each end of next and 2 foll 10th rows. 72 [76, 80, 84] sts.

Work 5 [9, 9, 11] rows straight.

Shape armholes

Cast off 7 [5, 3, 2] sts at beg of next 2 rows. 58 [66, 74, 80] sts.

Dec 1 st at each end of next 3 rows, then foll alt row. 50 [58, 66, 72] sts.

Cont straight until armhole meas 16.5 [17.5, 18.5, 19.5]cm, ending with RS facing for next row.

Shape shoulders

Cast off 3 [4, 5, 6] sts at beg of next 2 rows. 44 [50, 56, 60] sts.

Next row – Cast off 3 [4, 5, 6] sts, K until there are 8 [9, 10, 10] sts on right hand needle, turn and work this side first.

Next row – Cast off 4 sts, P to end.

Cast off rem 4 [5, 6, 6] sts.

With RS facing rejoin yarn to rem sts, cast off centre 22 [24, 26, 28] sts, K to end.

Complete to match first side reversing shapings.

LEFT FRONT

Work as given for Back to **.

Work 6 [10, 12, 16] rows straight, ending with WS facing for next row.

Shape neck

Next row – Cast off 2 sts, P to end. 64 [68, 72, 76] sts.

Work 32 rows inc 1 st at side edge in 7th [7th, 3rd, 1st] and 2 foll 10th of these rows at same time dec 1 st at neck edge in every row.
35 [39, 43, 47] sts.
Shape armhole
Next row – Cast off 7 [5, 3, 2] sts, K to last 2 sts, K2tog. 27 [33, 39, 44] sts.
Next row – Purl.
Dec 1 st at armhole edge (beg) in next 3 rows then foll alt row at same time dec 1 st at neck edge in next and every foll alt row.
20 [26, 32, 37] sts.
Dec 1 st at neck edge only in 2nd and every foll alt row to 18 [20, 21, 21] sts, then on every foll 4th row to 10 [13, 16, 18] sts.
Cont straight until left front matches Back to shoulder shaping, ending with RS facing for next row.
Shape shoulder
Cast off 3 [4, 5, 6] sts at beg of next and foll alt row.
Work 1 row more.
Cast off rem 4 [5, 6, 6] sts.

RIGHT FRONT
Work as given for Back to **.
Work 5 [9, 11, 15] rows straight, ending with RS facing for next row.
Shape neck
Next row – Cast off 2 sts, K to end. 64 [68, 72, 76] sts.
Work 1 row more.
Work 33 rows dec 1 st at neck edge in every row at same time inc 1 st at side edge in 7th [7th, 3rd, 1st] and 2 foll 10th of these rows.
34 [38, 42, 46] sts.
Shape armhole
Next row – (WS) Cast off 7 [5, 3, 2] sts, P to end.
27 [33, 39, 44] sts.
Complete to match Left front reversing shapings and working 1 row more before shoulder shaping.

SLEEVES (Both alike)
Using 5mm (USA 8) needles and yarn A, cast on 36 [38, 40, 42] sts.

Work first 34 rows of stripe sequence as set shaping sides by inc 1 st at each end of 5th and every foll 4th [6th, 6th, 6th] of these rows. 52 [48, 50, 52] sts.
Work rows 39 to 42 of stripe sequence inc 1 st at each end of 0 [1st, 1st, 1st] of these rows.
52 [50, 52, 54] sts.
Cont in yarn D only inc 1 st at each end of 1st [3rd, 3rd, 3rd] and every foll 6th row to 70 [72, 74, 66] sts.

Size 9/10 yrs only
Inc 1 st at each end of every foll 8th row to 76 sts.

All sizes
Cont straight until sleeve meas 33 [37, 41, 45]cm, ending with RS facing for next row.
Shape top
Cast off 7 [5, 3, 2] sts at beg of next 2 rows.
56 [62, 68, 72] sts.
Dec 1 st at each end of next 6 rows.
44 [50, 56, 60] sts.
Cast off 12 [15, 18, 20] sts at beg of next 2 rows.
Cast off rem 20 sts.

MAKING UP
Join shoulder seams.
Neck edging
With RS facing using 4½mm (USA 7) needles and yarn C, pick up and knit 54 [60, 66, 72] sts up right side of neck, 30 [32, 34, 36] sts from back of neck and 54 [60, 66, 72] sts down left side of neck. 138 [152, 166, 180] sts.
Work 2 rows in g st. Cast off.
Left front edging
With RS facing using 4½mm (USA 7) needles and yarn C, pick up and knit 41 [45, 49, 51] sts along left front edge. Work 2 rows in g st. Cast off.
Right front edging
Work as given for Left front edging.
Sew side seams and inset sleeves.
Ties (make 2)
Using yarn C and 5.00mm (USA H8) crochet hook, ch until tie meas 20cm.
Attach one to right front at start of neck shaping and

one at left side seam to correspond.
Make button loop on left immediately below start of
neck shaping.
Sew button to inside of seam to correspond.

EMBROIDERY

Using scraps of yarns A, B, C, E, F, embroider motifs
on front and sleeves using photograph as a guide.
Refer to Information page for stitching information.

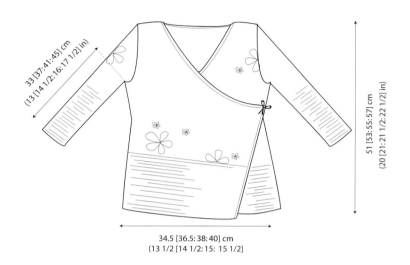

33 [37:41:45] cm
(13 [14 1/2:16:17 1/2] in)

51 [53:55:57] cm
(20 [21:21 1/2:22 1/2] in)

34.5 [36.5: 38: 40] cm
(13 1/2 [14 1/2: 15: 15 1/2])

Jay

Marie Wallin

Jay (left)

SIZE

	3/4	5/6	7/8	9/10	yrs

To fit chest

	55–57	59–61	63–67	69–73	cm

YARN

Rowan Handknit Cotton
Yarn A (Thunder 335)

	7	8	9	10	x 50g

Yarn B (Ice Water 239)

	1	1	1	1	x 50g

NEEDLES

1 pair 3¾mm (no 9) (USA 5) needles
1 pair 4mm (no 8) (USA 6) needles
Cable needle
Stitch holders
6 buttons – approx. 1.5cm – 1.75cm diameter
6 poppers

TENSION

20 sts and 28 rows to 10cm over st st on 4mm (USA 6) needles

SPECIAL ABBREVIATIONS

CN = cable needle
C6B = slip next 3 sts onto CN and hold at back of work, K3, then K3 from CN
C6F = slip next 3 sts onto CN and leave at front of work, K3, then K3 from CN

BACK

Using 3¾mm (USA 5) needles and yarn A, cast on 74 [78, 82, 86] sts.
Row 1 – (RS) * P2, K2, rep from * to last 2 sts, P2.
Row 2 – K2 * P2, K2, rep from * to end.
These 2 rows form 2x2 rib.
Work 10 rows more in rib, dec 2 sts evenly across last of these rows. 72 [76, 80, 84] sts.
Change to 4mm (USA 6) needles
Beg with a K row cont in st st until back meas 24 [25, 26, 27]cm, ending with RS facing for next row.
Shape armholes
Cast off 5 [4, 3, 2] sts at beg of next 2 rows.

62 [68, 74, 80] sts.
Dec 1 st at each end of next 3 rows, then 2 foll alt rows. 52 [58, 64, 70] sts.
Cont straight until armhole meas 15.5 [16.5, 17.5, 18.5]cm, ending with RS facing for next row.
Shape shoulders
Next row – Cast off 5 [6, 7, 8] sts, K until there are 7 [8, 9, 10] sts on right hand needle, turn and work this side first.
Next row – P2tog, P to end.
Cast off rem 6 [7, 8, 9] sts.
With RS facing cast off centre 28 [30, 32, 34] sts, K to end.
Complete to match first side reversing shapings.

LEFT FRONT

Using 3¾mm (USA 5) needles and yarn A, cast on 36 [36, 40, 40] sts.
Row 1 - * P2, K2, rep from * to end.
This row forms rib.
Work 11 rows more in rib dec 2 [0, 2, 0] sts evenly across last of these rows. 34 [36, 38, 40] sts.
Change to 4mm (USA 6) needles
Row 1 – (RS) K26 [28, 30, 32], P2, K6.
Row 2 – P6, K2, P26 [28, 30, 32].
Row 3 – K20 [22, 24, 26], C6B, P2, K6.
Row 4 – As row 2.
Row 5 – As row 1.
Row 6 – As row 2.
These 6 rows form patt.
Work 2 rows more in patt.
Next row – (RS) K12 [14, 16, 18], slip rem sts onto a stitch holder and cont on these 12 [14, 16, 18] sts only.
Next row – Beg with a P row work 23 rows in st st , leave these sts on second stitch holder and rejoin yarn to RS of rem 22 sts.
Work 24 rows in patt.
With RS facing rejoin yarn to sts left on second holder and working across all 34 [36, 38, 40] sts cont in patt until left front matches Back to armhole shaping, ending with RS facing for next row.
Shape armhole
Next row – Keeping patt correct, cast off 5 [4, 3, 2] sts, patt to end. 29 [32, 35, 38] sts.
Work 1 row more.

Dec 1 st at armhole edge in next 3 rows, then 2 foll alt rows. 24 [27, 30, 33] sts.
Cont straight until 13 [13, 13, 15] rows less have been worked than on Back to shoulder shaping, ending with WS facing for next row.
Shape neck
Next row – Cast off 5 [6, 7, 8] sts, patt to end.
19 [21, 23, 25] sts.
Work 1 row more.
Next row – Cast off 4 sts, patt to end 15 [17, 19, 21] sts.
Work 1 row more.
Dec 1 st at neck edge in next 2 rows then 2 foll alt rows. 11 [13, 15, 17] sts.
Cont straight until left front matches Back to shoulder shaping, ending with RS facing for next row.
Shape shoulder
Next row - Cast off 5 [6, 7, 8] sts, patt to end.
Work 1 row more.
Cast off rem 6 [7, 8, 9] sts.

RIGHT FRONT
Using 3¾mm (USA 5) needles and yarn A, cast on 36 [36, 40, 40] sts.
Row 1 - * K2, P2, rep from * to end.
This row forms rib.
Work 11 rows more in rib dec 2 [0, 2, 0] sts evenly across last of these rows. 34 [36, 38, 40] sts.
Change to 4mm (USA 6) needles
Row 1 – (RS) K6, P2, K26 [28, 30, 32]
Row 2 – P26 [28, 30, 32], K2, P6.
Row 3 – K6, P2, C6F, K20 [22, 24, 26].
Row 4 – As row 2.
Row 5 – As row 1.
Row 6 – As row 2.
These 6 rows form patt.
Work 2 rows in patt.
Next row – K6, P2, C6F, K8, slip rem sts onto a stitch holder and cont on these 22 sts only.
Work 23 rows in patt and leave these sts on a second stitch holder and rejoin yarn to RS of rem 12 [14, 16, 18] sts.
Beg with a K row work 24 rows in st st.
With RS facing rejoin to sts left on second holder and working across all 34 [36, 38, 38] sts work as given for Left front reversing shapings and working 1 row more

before armhole and shoulder shapings and 1 row less before neck shaping.

SLEEVES (Both alike)
Using 3¾mm (USA 5) needles and yarn A, cast on 38 [38, 42, 42] sts.
Work 10 rows in rib as given for Back, dec 2 [0, 2, 0] sts across last of these rows. 36 [38, 40, 42] sts.
Change to 4mm (USA 6) needles
Beg with a K row cont in st st shaping sides by inc 1 st at each end of 9th and every foll 6th [8th, 8th, 10th] row to 46 [58, 50, 62] sts.

Sizes 3/4 and 7/8 yrs only
Inc 1 st at each end of every foll 8th [-, 10th, -] row to 56 [-, 60, -] sts.

All sizes
Cont straight until sleeve meas 34 [38, 42, 46]cm, ending with RS facing for next row.
Shape top
Cast off 5 [4, 3, 2] sts at beg of next 2 rows.
46 [50, 54, 58] sts.
Dec 1 st at each end of next 3 rows, then on 2 foll alt rows. 36 [40, 44, 48] sts.
Work 1 row more.
Cast off 6 [8, 10, 12] sts at beg of next 2 rows. Cast off rem 24 sts.

MAKING UP
Join shoulder seams.
Mock pocket cuff (both alike)
Using 3¾mm (USA 5) needles and yarn B, pick up and knit 20 sts along pocket slit from fabric nearest cable.
Beg with a P row work 5 rows in st st.
Next row – (RS) Purl.
Next row – Knit.
Cast off purlwise.
Slip stitch row end edges to garment.
Left shoulder panel
Using 3¾mm (USA 5) needles and yarn B, cast on 14 [16, 18, 20] sts.
Row 1- (RS and front of shoulder) Purl.
Next row – Knit.
Next row - Purl.

With WS facing, beg with a P row work 6 rows in st st dec 1 st at end of 2nd and foll 4th of these rows.
12 [14, 16, 18] sts.
Work 3 [5, 7, 9] rows straight.
Inc 1 st at end of next and foll 4th row. 14 [16, 18, 20] sts.
Work 1 row more.
Next row – (RS) Purl.
Next row – Knit.
Cast off purlwise.

Right shoulder panel
Work to match Left shoulder panel reversing shapings.
Pin in place with equal amounts over front and back shoulders.
Insert sleeves at the same time catching in row end edges of shoulder panels.

Right front edging
With RS facing using 3¾mm (USA 5) needles and yarn A, pick up and knit 94 [98, 102, 106] sts evenly along front edge.
Row 1 – (WS) P2, * K2, P2, rep from * to end.
Row 2 - * K2, P2, rep from * to last 2 sts, K2.
Rep last 2 rows 3 times more.
Cast off in rib.
Place button markers, the first to be 4cm from top edge, the last to be 4cm from bottom edge and 3 to be evenly spaced between.

Left front edging
Work as given for right front edging.

Collar
With RS facing using 3¾mm (USA5) needles and yarn A pick up and knit 22 [22, 22, 24] sts across band and up right neck edge, 30 [34, 38, 42] sts from back neck and 22 [22, 22, 24] sts down left side of neck and band (picking up sts from shoulder panel at same time).
74 [78, 82, 90] sts.
Work 15 rows in rib as given for right front edging.
Cast off in rib.
Using yarn A double work running stitch along front and back shoulder panels using photograph as a guide.

Covered buttons (make 6)
Using 3¾mm (USA 5) needles and yarn B, cast on 3 sts.
Beg with a K row cont in st st inc 1 st at each end of next 2 rows. 7 sts.
Work 3 rows straight.
Dec 1 st at each end of next 2 rows. 3 sts. Cast off.
Encase button in knitting.
Join side and sleeve seams and sew buttons and poppers onto garment.

EMBROIDERY
Using oddments of yarn A, embroider a running stitch along shoulder panel. See photograph for reference.

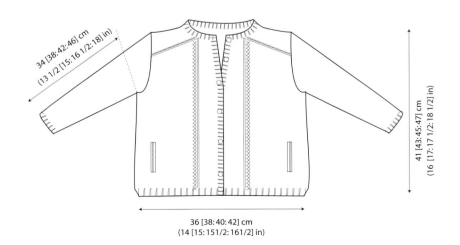

34 [38: 42: 46] cm
(13 1/2 [15: 16 1/2: 18] in)

41 [43: 45: 47] cm
(16 [17: 17 1/2: 18 1/2] in)

36 [38: 40: 42] cm
(14 [15: 151/2: 161/2] in)

Kate Greenaway

Wendi

P.16 Cushions   7½in squares   Aniving 18

P26   Scented   Sachets   Victorian P 65

P86   Miniatures   Brass frames   Rose

Flowers in X Stitch   Chris

   P 14   Roses Bell pull   25 linen

Samplers

P.32. Friendship   Mattie

    Jo Verso.

P52   The Things I Sow -   Sue A

25·6·17.

£61

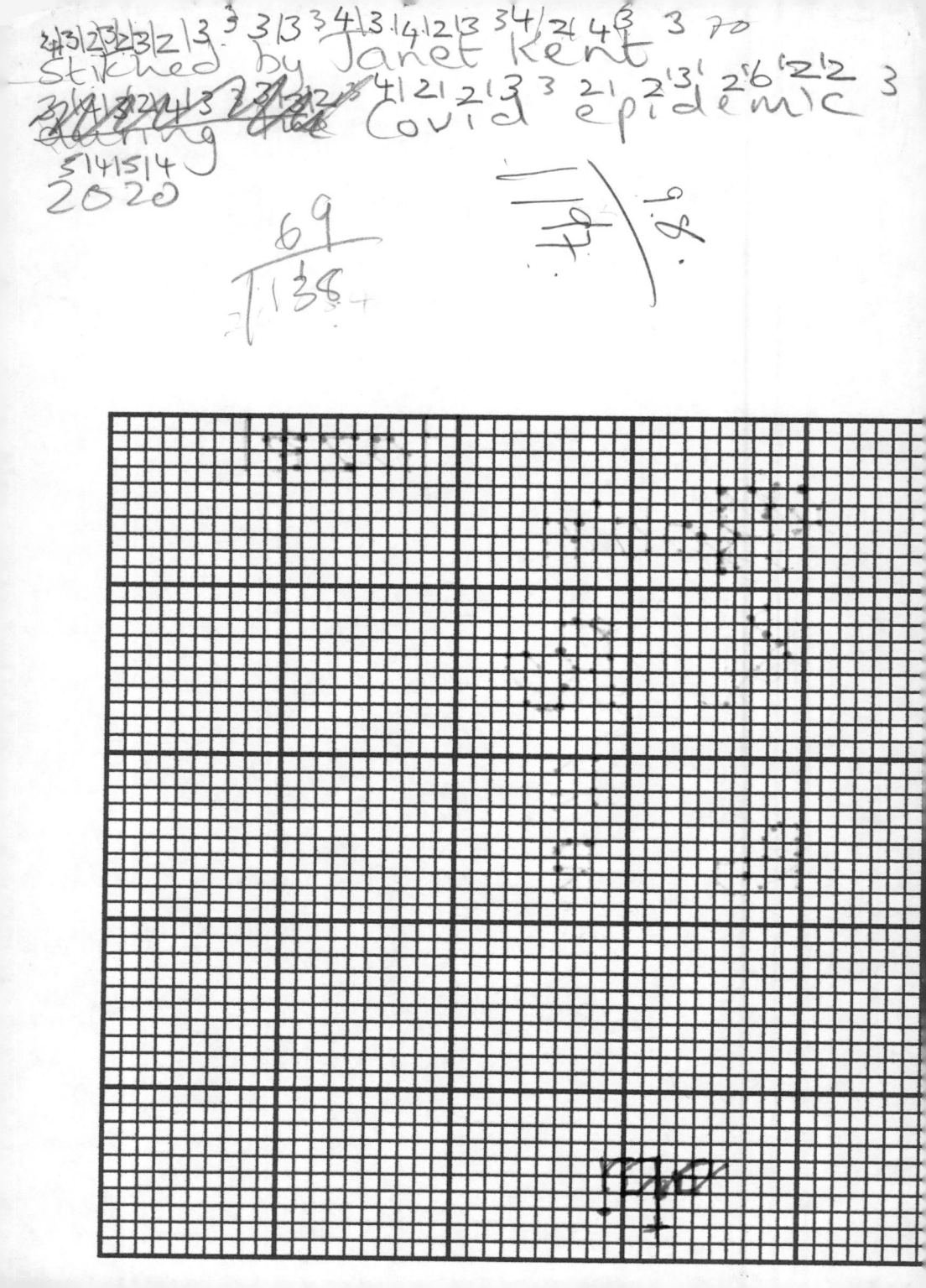

Stiched by Janet Kent
during the Covid epidemic
2020

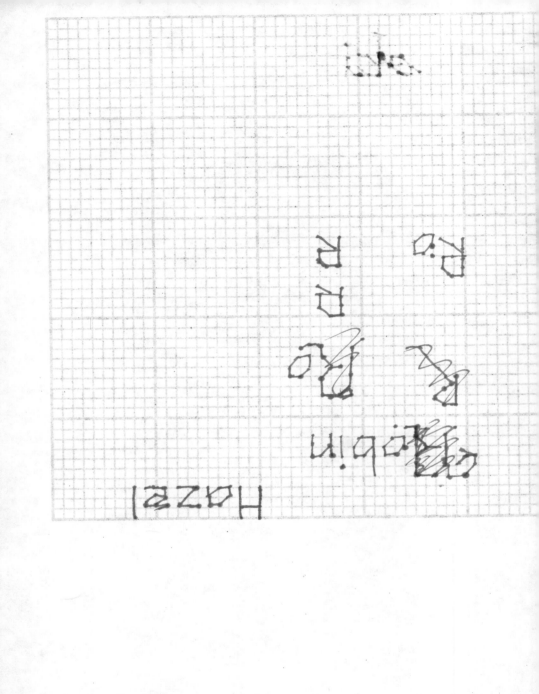

Brambling

Marie Wallin

SIZE

	3/4	5/6	7/8	9/10	yrs

To fit chest

	55–57	59–61	63–67	69–73	cm

YARN

Rowan All Seasons Cotton (Jersey 191)

	6	7	8	9	x 50g

NEEDLES

1 pair 4½mm (no 7) (USA 7) needles
Cable needles
4 x 00417 buttons
13 x 00416 buttons

TENSION

18 sts and 25 rows to 10cm over st st on 4½mm (USA 7) needles

SPECIAL ABBREVIATIONS

CN=cable needle
6B=slip next 6 sts onto CN and leave at back of work.
PtogCN=purl together 1 st from CN and 1 st from left hand needle.

BACK

Using 4½mm (USA 7) needles cast on 83 [87, 91, 95] sts.
Row 1 – (RS) Purl.
Row 2 – Knit.
Beg with a K row work 22 rows in st st shaping sides by dec 1 st at each end of 3rd and every foll 4th of these rows. 73 [77, 81, 85] sts.
Next row – K2tog, K16 [18, 20, 22], 6B, K25, 6B, K16 [18, 20, 22], K2tog. 71 [75, 79, 83] sts.
Next row – P11 [13, 15, 17], (PtogCN) 6 times, P25, (PtogCN) 6 times, P11 [13, 15, 17]. 59 [63, 67, 71] sts.

Pattern panels
Row 1 – (RS) K15 [17, 19, 21], P2, K25, P2, K15 [17, 19, 21].
Row 2 – P15 [17, 19, 21], K2, P25, K2, P15 [17, 19, 21].
Row 3 – K2tog, K to last 2 sts, K2tog. 57 [61, 65, 69] sts.
Row 4 – Purl.
These 4 rows set position of patt panels.
Cont in patt shaping sides by dec 1 st at each end of

3rd row and inc 1 st at each end of 3 foll 4th [4th, 6th, 6th] rows. 61 [65, 69, 73] sts.
Cont in patt working straight until back meas 21 [22, 23, 24]cm, ending with RS facing for next row.

Shape armholes
Cast off 4 [3, 2, 1] sts at beg of next 2 rows.
53 [59, 65, 71] sts.
Dec 1 st at each end of next 3 rows, then foll alt row.
45 [51, 57, 63] sts.
Cont straight until armhole meas 15.5 [16.5, 17.5, 18.5]cm, ending with RS facing for next row.

Shape shoulders
Cast off 3 [4, 4, 5] sts, at beg of next 2 rows.
39 [43, 49, 53] sts.
Next row – Cast off 3 [4, 5, 5] sts, K until there are 7 [7, 8, 9] sts on right hand needle, turn and work this side first.
Next row – Cast off 3 sts, P to end.
Cast off rem 4 [4, 5, 6] sts.
With RS facing rejoin yarn to rem sts, cast off centre 19 [21, 23, 25] sts, K to end.
Complete to match first side reversing shapings.

LEFT FRONT

Using 4½mm (USA 7) needles cast on 55 [57, 59, 61] sts.
Row 1 – (RS) Purl.
Row 2 – Knit.
Row 3 – K to last 2 sts, P2.
Row 4 – K2, P to end.
Rows 3 and 4 form patt.
Work 20 rows in patt shaping sides by dec 1 st at side edge (beg) in next and every foll 4th of these rows.
50 [52, 54, 56] sts.
Next row – K2tog, K10 [12, 14, 16], * 6B, K6, rep from * twice more, P2. 49 [51, 53, 55] sts. (Place marker on this row to denote first button).
Next row – K2, P6, ** (PtogCN) 6 times, rep from ** twice more, P5 [7, 9, 11]. 31 [33, 35, 37] sts.

Pattern panel
Row 1 – (RS) K9 [11, 13, 15], (P2, K4) twice, P2, K6, P2.
Row 2 – K2, P6, (K2, P4) twice, K2, P9 [11, 13, 15].
Row 3 – K2tog, K to last 2 sts, P2. 30 [32, 34, 36] sts.
Row 4 – K2, P to end.
These 4 rows set position of patt panels.
Cont in patt shaping side by dec 1 st at side edge in

3rd row and inc 1 st at side edge in 3 foll 4th [4th, 6th, 6th] rows. 32 [34, 36, 38] sts.
Cont in patt working straight until left front matches Back to armhole shaping, ending with RS facing for next row.
Shape armhole
Next row – Cast off 4 [3, 2, 1] sts, patt to end. 28 [31, 34, 37] sts.
Work 1 row more.
Dec 1 st at armhole edge (beg) of next 3 rows, then foll alt row. 24 [27, 30, 33] sts.
Cont in patt working straight until 15 rows less have been worked than on Back to shoulder shaping, ending with WS facing for next row.
Shape neck
Next row – Cast off 8 [9, 10, 11] sts, patt to end. 16 [18, 20, 22] sts.
Dec 1 st at neck edge in next 3 rows then 3 foll alt rows. 10 [12, 14, 16] sts.
Cont straight until left front matches Back to shoulder shaping, ending with RS facing for next row.
Shape shoulder
Cast off 3 [4, 4, 5] sts at beg of next row and 3 [4, 5, 5] sts at beg of foll alt row.
Work 1 row more.
Cast off rem 4 [4, 5, 6] sts.
Place rem 3 button markers, the second to be at neck edge and 2 more spaced evenly in between.

RIGHT FRONT
Using 4½mm (USA 7) needles cast on 55 [57, 59, 61] sts.
Row 1 – (RS) Purl.
Row 2 – Knit.
Row 3 – P2, K to end.
Row 4 – P to last 2 sts, K2.
Rows 3 and 4 form patt.
Work 20 rows in patt shaping side by dec 1 st at side edge (end) in next and every foll 4th of these rows. 50 [52, 54, 56] sts.
Next row (Buttonhole row) – P2, cast off 2 sts, (2 sts to be cast on over these sts on next row), K3, * 6B, K6, rep from * once, 6B, K10 [12, 14, 16], K2tog. 49 [51, 53, 55] sts.
Next row – P5 [7, 9, 11], ** (PtogCN) 6 times, rep from ** twice more, P6, K2. 31 [33, 35, 37] sts.

Pattern panel
Row 1 – (RS) P2, K6, (P2, K4) twice, P2, K9 [11, 13, 15].
Row 2 –P9 [11, 13, 15], (K2, P4) twice, K2, P6, K2.
Row 3 – P2, K to last 2 sts, K2tog. 30 [32, 34, 36] sts.
Row 4 – P to last 2sts, K2.
These 4 rows set position of patt panels.
Complete to match left front reversing shapings, working 1 row less before armhole and shoulder shaping and 1 row more before neck shaping and working 3 more buttonholes to correspond with markers.

SLEEVES (Both alike)
Using 4½mm (USA 7) needles cast on 32 [34, 36, 38] sts.
Row 1 – (RS of sleeve WS of cuff) Knit.
Row 2 – Purl.
Beg with a P row, work 8 rows in rev st st.
Turn back cuff is now complete.
Beg with a K row cont in st st shaping sides by inc 1 st at each end of 11th row and every foll 8th [10th, 10th, 10th] row to 44 [46, 48, 50] sts.
Work 7 [7, 9, 11] rows straight, ending with RS facing for next row.
Next row – Purl.
Next row – Knit.
Beg with a K row and cont in st st inc 1 st at each end of next and foll 10th [10th, 12th, 14th] row. 48 [50, 52, 54] sts.
Cont straight until sleeve meas 33 [37, 41, 45]cm (excluding turn back of cuff), ending with RS facing for next row.
Shape top
Cast off 4 [3, 2, 1] sts at beg of next 2 rows. 40 [44, 48, 52] sts.
Dec 1 st at each end of next 6 rows. 28 [32, 36, 40] sts.
Cast off 8 [10, 12, 14] sts at beg of next 2 rows.
Cast off rem 12 sts.

MAKING UP
Join shoulder and side seams.
Collar
Using 4½mm (USA 7) needles cast on 61 [65, 69, 73] sts.
Purl 2 rows.
Beg with a K row and working in st st throughout work 2 rows.

Cast off 3 sts at beg of next 16 rows.

Cast off rem 13 [17, 21, 25] sts.

Sew shaped edge of collar to neck edge. Fold collar in half to RS and slip stitch cast on edge to garment.

Pocket

Using 4½mm (USA 7) needles cast on 14 sts.

Beg with a K row cont in st st until pocket meas 7cm, ending with RS facing for next row.

Next row – Purl.

Cast off.

Slip stitch pocket onto left sleeve using photograph as a guide and sew on small button.

Join sleeve seams. Insert sleeves.

Back tie (Make 2)

Using 4½mm (USA 7) needles cast on 8 sts.

Beg with a K row cont in st st until tie meas 16cm, ending with RS facing for next row.

Work 7 rows dec 1 st at same edge in every row.

Fasten off.

Sew straight edge of each tie to inside edge of back pattern panels using photograph as a guide.

Sew 1 small button to base of each pattern panel.

Sew large buttons to left front edge.

Turn back cuffs and sew 2 small buttons to each cuff.

33 [37:41:45] cm
(13 [14 1/2: 16:17 1/2] in)

39 [41:43:45] cm
(16 1/2 [16:17:171/2] in)

34 [36: 38 .5: 40.5] cm
(14 [14: 15: 16] in)

Robin

Marie Wallin

SIZE

	3/4	5/6	7/8	9/10	yrs

To fit chest

55–57   59–61   63–67   69–73   cm

YARN

Rowan Handknit Cotton
Yarn A (Tope 253)

	3	4	4	5	x 50g

Yarn B (Linen 205)

	4	4	5	5	x 50g

Yarn C (Raffia 330)

	2	2	2	2	x 50g

NEEDLES

1 pair 4mm (no 8) (USA 6) needles
1 pair 3¾mm (no 9) (USA 5) needles
1 x 3¾mm (USA 5) short circular needle (or set of
4 double pointed needles)
Stitch holder

TENSION

20 sts and 28 rows to 10cm over st st and 26 sts and
28 rows over rib on 4mm (USA 6) needles

BACK

Using 3¾mm (USA 5) needles and yarn A, cast on
94 [98, 102, 106] sts.
Row 1 – * K2, P2, rep from * to last 2 sts, K2.
Row 2 – P2, * K2, P2, rep from * to end.
These 2 rows form 2x2 rib.
Work 8 rows more in rib.
Change to 4mm (USA 6) needles
Cont in rib until back meas 24 [25, 26, 27]cm, ending
with RS facing for next row.
Shape armholes
Keeping rib correct cast off 6 sts at beg of next 2 rows.
82 [86, 90, 94] sts.

Dec 1 st at each end of next 5 rows then foll alt row.
70 [74, 78, 82] sts.
Cont straight until armhole meas 15.5 [16.5,
17.5, 18.5]cm, ending with RS facing for next row.
Shape shoulders
Next row - Cast off 8 [8, 9, 9] sts **at same time** dec
2 sts evenly across cast off sts, patt until there are
15 [16, 16, 17] sts on right hand needle, turn and work
this side first.
Next row – Cast off 7 sts , patt to end.
Cast off rem 8 [9, 9, 10] sts, **at same time** dec 2 sts
evenly across these cast off sts.
With RS facing, cast off centre 24 [26, 28, 30] sts **at
same time** dec 6 sts evenly across these sts, K to end.
Complete to match first side reversing shapings.

FRONT

Using 3¾mm (USA 5) needles and yarn A cast on
70 [74, 78, 82] sts.
Work 10 rows in rib as given for Back.
Change to 4mm (USA 6) needles and yarn B.
Beg with a K row, working in st st throughout, work
6 rows in yarn B and six rows in yarn C.
These 12 rows form stripe sequence.
Cont in stripe sequence, until front matches Back to
armhole shaping, ending with RS facing for next row.
Shape armholes
Keeping stripe patt correct cast off 4 sts at beg of next
2 rows. 62 [66, 70, 74] sts.
Dec 1 st at each end of next 3 rows then on foll alt row.
54 [58, 62, 66] sts.
Cont straight until 12 [12, 12, 14] rows less have been
worked than on back to shoulder shaping, ending with
RS facing for next row.
Shape neck
Next row – K21 [23, 25, 27], turn and work this side
first.
Next row – Cast off 4 [5, 6, 7] sts, P to end.
17 [18, 19, 20] sts.

Work 1 row more.
Dec 1 st at neck edge in next 3 rows, then in 2 foll alt rows. 12 [13, 14, 15] sts.
Cont straight until front matches Back to shoulder shaping, ending with RS facing for next row.

Shape shoulder
Next row – Cast off 6 [6, 7, 7] sts, K to end.
Work 1 row more.
Cast off rem 6 [7, 7, 8] sts.
With RS slip centre 12 sts onto a stitch holder, rejoin yarn to rem sts, K to end.
Complete to match first side reversing shapings and working 1 row more before shoulder shaping.

SLEEVES (Both alike)
Using 3¾mm (USA 5) needles and yarn A, cast on 40 [44, 44, 48] sts.
Row 1 – (RS) K1, P2, * K2, P2, rep from * to last st, K1.
Row 2 – P1, * K2, P2, rep from * to last 3 sts, K2, P1.
These 2 rows form rib.
Work 8 rows more in rib dec 0 [2, 0, 2] sts evenly across last of these rows. 40 [42, 44, 46] sts.
Change to 4mm (USA 6) needles and yarn B
Row 1 – (RS) K11 [12, 13, 14], P2, (K2, P2) 4 times, K11 [12, 13, 14].
Row 2 – P11 [12, 13, 14], (K2, P2) 4 times, K2, P11 [12, 13, 14].
These 2 rows set rib patt and st st.
Cont as set shaping sides by inc 1 st at each end of 5th and every foll 4th [6th, 6th, 6th] row to 46 [66, 58, 56] sts.

Size 3/4, 7/8 and 9/10 yrs only
Inc 1 st at each end of every foll 6th [-, 8th, 8th] row to 64 [-, 68, 70] sts.

All sizes
Cont straight until sleeve meas 31 [33, 37, 39]cm, ending with RS facing for next row.

Shape top
Keeping stripe patt correct cast off 4 sts at beg of next 2 rows. 56 [58, 60, 62] sts.
Dec 1 st at each end of next 4 rows. 48 [50, 52, 54] sts.
Cast off 5 [5, 6, 6] sts at beg of next 2 rows.
38 [40, 40, 42] sts.
Cast off 8 [9, 9, 10] sts at beg of next 2 rows.
Cast off rem 22 sts.

MAKING UP
Join shoulder, side and sleeve seams.
Left shoulder panel
Using 3¾mm (USA 5) needles and yarn C cast on 14 [15, 16, 17] sts.
Row 1 – (RS and front of shoulder) Purl.
Row 2 – Knit.
Row 3 – Purl.
With WS facing beg with a P row, work 16 [16, 16, 18] rows in st st dec 1 st at end of 2nd and foll 4th row.
12 [13, 14, 15] sts.
Work 5 rows straight.
Inc 1 st at end of next and foll 4th row.
14 [15, 16, 17] sts.
Work 1 row more.
Next row – (RS) Purl.
Next row – Knit.
Cast off purlways.
Right shoulder panel
Work to match Left shoulder panel reversing shapings.
Pin in place with equal amounts over front and back shoulder.
Insert sleeves also catching in row end edges of shoulder panels.
Neckband
With RS facing using 3¾mm (USA 5) circular needle and yarn A, pick up and knit 22 [22, 22, 23] sts down left side of neck, K across 12 sts left on a stitch holder at front neck, pick up and knit 22 [22, 22, 23] sts up right side of neck and 36 [40, 40, 42] sts from back of

neck (picking up sts from shoulder panel at same time across both shoulders).
92 [96, 96, 100] sts.
Working in rounds:-
Round 1 - * K2, P2, rep from * to end.

Work a further 7 rounds.
Cast off in rib.
Using yarn B work running stitches around neck edge and along front edges of shoulder panels using photograph as a guide.

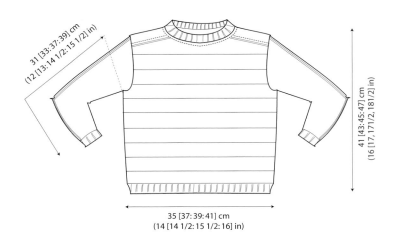

31 [33:37:39] cm
(12 [13:14 1/2: 15 1/2] in)

41 [43:45:47] cm
(16 [17, 171/2, 181/2] in)

35 [37: 39: 41] cm
(14 [14 1/2: 15 1/2: 16] in)

Serin

Marie Wallin

SIZE

	3/4	5/6	7/8	9/10	yrs

To fit chest

	55–57	59–61	63–67	69–73	cm

YARN

Rowan All Seasons Cotton
Yarn A (Jersey 191)

	6	6	7	8	x 50g

Yarn B (Iceberg 192)

	1	1	1	1	x 50g

NEEDLES

1 pair 4½mm (no 7) (USA 7) needles
1 pair 4mm (no 8) (USA 6) needles
3 x 00410 buttons

TENSION

18 sts and 25 rows to 10cm over st st on 4½mm (USA 7) needles

Stripe sequence

Row 1 –P using yarn B
Row 2 – K using yarn B
Row 3 – P using yarn B
Row 4 – K using yarn A
Row 5 – As row 4
Row 6 – P using yarn A
Rows 7 to 10 – Rep rows 5 and 6 twice
Row 11 – P using yarn B
Row 12 – K using yarn B
Row 13 – P using yarn B
Row 14 – K using yarn A

BACK

Using 4½mm (USA 7) needles and yarn A, cast on 62 [64, 68, 72] sts.
Row 1 – (RS) Purl.
Row 2 – Knit.
Beg with a K row work 24 rows st st shaping sides by dec 1 st at each end of 15th and foll 6th row.
58 [60, 64, 68] sts.

Work 14 rows of stripe sequence dec1 st at each end of 3rd and inc 1 st at each end of 13th of these rows.
58 [60, 64, 68] sts.
Cont in st st using yarn A only, inc 1 st at each end of 5th and foll 6th row.
62 [64, 68, 72] sts.
Cont in straight until back meas 22 [23, 24, 25]cm, ending with RS facing for next row.
Shape armholes
Cast off 3 [2, 2, 2] sts at beg of next 2 rows.
56 [60, 64, 68] sts.
Dec 1 st at each end of next 3 rows, then 2 [2, 1, 1] foll alt rows. 46 [50, 56, 60] sts.
Cont straight until armhole meas 15.5 [16.5, 17.5, 18.5]cm, ending with RS facing for next row.
Shape shoulders
Next row – Cast off 5 [5, 6, 7] sts, K until there are 8 [9, 10, 10] sts on right hand needle, turn and work this side first.
Next row – Cast off 3 sts, P to end.
Cast off rem 5 [6, 7, 7] sts.
With RS facing rejoin yarn A to rem sts, cast off centre 20 [22, 24, 26] sts, K to end.
Complete to match first side reversing shapings.

LEFT FRONT

Using 4½mm (USA 7) needles and yarn A, cast on 36 [37, 39, 41] sts.
Row 1 – (RS) Purl.
Row 2 – Knit.
Row 3 – K26 [27, 29, 31], P2, K6, P2.
Row 4 – K2, P6, K2, P26 [27, 29, 31].
Rows 3 and 4 set st st with button band patt.
Work 22 rows more in patt shaping side by dec 1 st at side edge (beg) in 13th and foll 6th of these rows.
34 [35, 37, 39] sts.
Work 14 rows of stripe sequence on first 24 [25, 27, 29] sts and button band patt as set using yarn A only on last 10 sts, dec 1 st at side edge (beg) in 3rd and inc 1 st at same edge in 13th of these rows.
34 [35, 37, 39] sts.
Cont in st st with band patt using yarn A only, inc 1 st at side edge in 5th and foll 6th of these rows.

36 [37, 39, 41] sts.
Cont straight until left front matches Back to armhole shaping, ending with RS facing for next row.

Shape armhole
Next row – Cast off 3 [2, 2, 2] sts, K to end.
33 [35, 37, 39] sts.
Work 1 row more.
Dec 1 st at armhole edge (beg) of next 3 rows, then 2 [2, 1, 1] foll alt rows. 28 [30, 33, 35] sts.
Cont straight until 10 rows less have been worked than on Back to shoulder shaping, ending with RS facing for next row.

Shape neck
Next row – K16 [17, 19, 20], cast off rem 12 [13, 14, 15]sts.
With WS facing rejoin yarn A to rem sts, P to end.
Dec 1 st at neck edge in next 5 rows, then foll alt row. 10 [11, 13, 14] sts.
Cont straight until left front matches Back to shoulder shaping, ending with RS facing for next row.

Shape shoulder
Next row – Cast off 5 [5, 6, 7] sts, K to end.
Work 1 row more.
Cast off rem 5 [6, 7, 7] sts.
Mark position of buttons - the first to be 3 rows below neck shaping, the third to be immediately above stripe sequence and the second to be halfway between.

RIGHT FRONT
Using 4½mm (USA 7) needles and yarn A cast on 36 [37, 39, 41] sts.
Row 1 – (RS) Purl.
Row 2 – Knit.
Row 3 – P2, K6, P2, K26 [27, 29, 31].
Row 4 – P26 [27, 29, 31], K2, P6, K2.
Rows 3 and 4 set button band patt and st st.
Work 22 rows more in patt shaping side by dec 1 st at side edge (end) in 13th and foll 6th of these rows.
34 [35, 37, 39] sts.
Work 14 rows of button band patt as set in yarn A only on first 10 sts and stripe sequence on last 24 [25, 27, 29] sts, dec 1 st at side edge in 3rd and inc 1 st at same edge in 13th of these rows.

34 [35, 37, 39] sts.
Cont to match Left front reversing shapings and working 1 row more before armhole, shoulder and neck shaping and working buttonholes to match markers as follows:-
Buttonhole row – P2, K2, cast off 2 sts, (2 sts to be cast on over these sts on next row), K1, P2, K to end.

SLEEVES (Both alike)
Using 4½mm (USA 7) needles and yarn A, cast on 32 [34, 36, 38] sts.
Row 1 – (RS) Purl.
Row 2 – Knit.
Beg with a K row work 6 rows in st st shaping sides by inc 1 st at each end of 5th of these rows.
34 [36, 38, 40] sts.
Work 34 rows in stripe sequence working rows 1-10 3 times, then rows 11-14 once, inc 1 st at each end of 5th and every foll 6th [6th, 8th, 8th] of these rows.
44 [46, 46, 48] sts.
Cont in st st using yarn A only inc 1 st at each end of 1st [3rd, 5th, 5th] and every foll 6th [8th, 8th, 8th] row to 54 [56, 58, 52] sts.

Size 9/10 yrs only
Inc 1 st at each end of every foll 10th row to 60 sts.

All sizes
Cont straight until sleeve meas 32 [36, 40, 44]cm, ending with RS facing for next row.

Shape top
Cast off 3 [2, 2, 2] sts at beg of next 2 rows.
48 [52, 54, 56] sts.
Dec 1 st at each end of next 6 rows.
36 [40, 42, 44] sts.
Cast off 12 [14, 15, 16] sts at beg of next 2 rows.
Cast off rem 12 sts.

MAKING UP
Join shoulder seams.
Neck edging
With RS facing, using 4mm (USA 8) needles and yarn A,

pick up and knit 19 sts up right side of neck, 25 [27, 29, 31] sts from back of neck and 19 sts down left side of neck. 63 [65, 67, 69] sts.
Next row – (WS) Knit.

Next row – Purl.
Next row – Knit. Cast off.
Join side and sleeve seams. Insert sleeves.
Sew on buttons.

32 [36:40:44] cm
(13 [14 1/2:16:17 1/2] in)

39 [41:43:45] cm
(15 1/2 [16:17:17 1/2] in)

34.5 [35.5: 38: 40] cm
(13 1/2 [14: 15: 16] in)

Sparrow
Marie Wallin

SIZE

	3/4	5/6	7/8	9/10	yrs
To fit chest					
	55–57	59–61	63–67	69–73	cm

YARN

Rowan Handknit Cotton
Yarn A (Rose 332)

	8	9	9	10	x 50g
Yarn B (Nectar 326)					
	1	1	1	1	x 50g
Yarn C (Aqua 327)					
	2	2	2	2	x 50g
Yarn D (Soap 331)					
	3	3	3	3	x 50g

NEEDLES

1 pair 4mm (no 8) (USA 6) needles
1 x 4.00mm (no 8) (USA G6) crochet hook

TENSION

22.5 sts and 28 rows to 10cm over pattern on 4mm
(USA 6) needles

CROCHET ABBREVIATIONS

ch = chain; ss = slip stitch; dc = double crochet;
tr = treble crochet; tog = together; dtr3tog = double
treble 3 together; tr3tog = treble 3 together

BACK

Using 4mm (USA 6) needles and yarn A, cast on
86 [92, 98, 104] sts.
Row1 – (RS) K2, * P1, yon, K2togtbl, P1, K2, rep from
* to end.
Row 2 – P2, * K1, P2, rep from * to end.
Row 3 – K2, * P1, K2tog, yrn, P1, K2, rep from * to end.
Row 4 – As row 2.
These 4 rows form patt.
Cont in patt shaping sides by dec 1 st at each end of
17th and every foll 14th [14th, 12th, 10th] row to

78 [84, 88, 92] sts.
Cont straight until back meas 28 [29, 30, 31]cm,
ending with RS facing for next row.
Shape armholes
Keeping patt correct, cast off 5 [4, 3, 2] sts at beg of
next 2 rows. 68 [76, 82, 88] sts.
Dec 1 st at each end of next 3 rows, then 2 foll alt
rows. 58 [66, 72, 78] sts.
Cont straight until armhole meas 15.5 [16.5,
17.5, 18.5]cm, ending with RS facing for next row.
Shape shoulders
Next row – Cast off 6 [7, 8, 9] sts, K9 [10, 11, 12], turn
and work this side first.
Next row – Cast off 3 sts, patt to end.
Cast off rem 6 [7, 8, 9] sts.
With RS facing rejoin yarn to rem sts, cast off centre
28 [32, 34, 36] sts, patt to end.
Complete to match first side reversing shapings.

LEFT FRONT

Using 4mm (USA 6) needles and yarn A, cast on
44 [46, 48, 50] sts.
Row 1 – K2, * P1, yon, K2togtbl, P1, K2, rep from * to
last 0 [2, 4, 0] sts, (P1, yon, K2togtbl) 0 [0, 1, 0] times,
P0 [1, 1, 0], K0 [1, 0, 0].
Row 2 – P2 [1, 0, 2] * K1, P2, rep from * to end.
Row 3 – K2, * P1, K2tog, yrn, P1, K2, rep from * to
last 0 [2, 4, 0] sts, (P1, K2tog, yrn) 0 [0, 1, 0] times,
P0 [1, 1, 0], K0 [1, 0, 0].
Row 4 – As row 2.
These 2 rows form patt.
Cont in patt shaping side by dec 1 st at side edge (beg)
in 17th and every foll 14th [14th, 12th, 10th] row to
40 [42, 43, 44] sts.
Cont straight until left front matches Back to armhole
shaping, ending with RS facing for next row.
Shape armhole
Next row – Cast off 5 [4, 3, 2] sts, patt to end.
35 [38, 40, 42] sts.
Work 1 row more.
Dec 1 st at armhole edge in next 3 rows, then 2 foll alt

rows. 30 [33, 35, 37] sts.
Cont straight until 33 rows less have been worked
than on Back to shoulder shaping, ending with WS
facing for next row.

Shape neck
Next row – Cast off 6 [7, 7, 7] sts, patt to end.
24 [26, 28, 30] sts.
Dec 1 st at neck edge in next 3, rows then foll 9 alt
rows. 12 [14, 16, 18] sts.
Cont straight until left front matches Back to shoulder
shaping, ending with RS facing for next row.

Shape shoulder
Next row – Cast off 6 [7, 8, 9] sts, patt to end.
Work 1 row more.
Cast off rem 6 [7, 8, 9] sts.

RIGHT FRONT
Using 4mm (USA 6) needles and yarn A, cast on
44 [46, 48, 50] sts.
Row 1 – (RS) K0 [1, 0, 0], P0 [1, 1, 0], (yon, K2togtbl,
P1) 0 [0, 1, 0] time, * K2, P1, yon, K2togtbl, P1, rep
from * to last 2 sts K2.
Row 2 – P2, * K1, P2, rep from * to last 0 [2, 1, 0] sts,
K 0 [1, 1, 0] P0 [1, 0, 0].
Row 3 – K0 [1, 0, 0], P0 [1, 1, 0], K0 [1, 0], (K2tog, yrn,
P1) 0 [0, 1, 0] time, * K2, P1, K2tog, yrn, P1, rep from
* to last 2 sts, K2.
Row 4 - As row 2.
These 4 rows set patt.
Complete to match Left front reversing shapings and
working 1 row more before armhole and shoulder
shaping and 1 row less before neck shaping.

SLEEVES (Both alike)
Using 4mm (USA 6) needles and yarn A, cast on
58 [60, 62, 64] sts.
Row 1 – (RS) K0 [1, 2, 0], P1 [1, 1, 0], K2 [2, 2, 0], * P1,
yon, K2togtbl, P1, K2, rep from * to last 1 [2, 3, 4] sts,
P1, K0 [1, 2, 0], (yon, K2togtbl, P1) 0 [0, 0, 1] time.
Row 2 – P0 [1, 2, 0], K1, * P2, K1, rep from * to last
0 [1, 2, 0] sts, P0 [1, 2, 0].

Row 3 – K0 [1, 2, 0], P1 [1, 1, 0], K2 [2, 2, 0], * P1,
K2tog, yrn, P1, K2, rep from * to last 1 [2, 3, 4] sts, P1,
K0 [1, 2, 0], (k2tog, yrn, P1) 0 [0, 0, 1] time.
Row 4 – As row 2.
These 4 rows form patt.
Cont in patt shaping sides by dec 1 st at each end
of 7th [11th, 13th, 15th] and 3 foll 8th [10th,
10th,10th] rows.
50 [52, 54, 56] sts.
Work 7 [7, 11, 11] rows straight.
Inc 1 st at each end of next and every foll 4th row to
72 [74, 76, 70] sts, working inc sts in patt.

Size 9/10 yrs only
Inc 1 st at each end of every foll 6th row to 78 sts.

All sizes
Cont straight until sleeve meas 33 [37, 41, 45]cm,
ending with RS facing for next row.

Shape top
Keeping patt correct, cast off 5 [4, 3, 2] sts at beg of
next 2 rows. 62 [66, 70, 74] sts.
Dec 1 st at each end of next 3 rows, then 2 foll
alt rows. 52 [56, 60, 64] sts.
Work 1 row.
Cast off 10 [12, 14, 16] sts at beg of next 2 rows
Cast off rem 32 sts.

MAKING UP
Join side, shoulder and sleeve seams. Insert sleeves.
5 petal Flower (make 31)
Using 4.00mm (USA G6) hook and yarn D, make 7ch,
ss to first ch to form a ring.
Round 1 – 1 ch, 14dc into ring, ss in first ch.
Round 2 – 4ch, *dtr4tog, inserting hook twice in next
dc and twice in foll dc, 3ch, 1dc into next dc, 3ch, rep
from * 3 times more, dtr4tog, inserting hook as before,
3ch, ss into first ch. Fasten off.
4 petal flower (make 31)
Using 4.00mm (USA G6) hook and yarn C, make 4ch,
ss into first ch to form a ring.

Round 1 – 1ch, 7dc into ring, ss in first ch.
Round 2 – (3ch, tr3tog all in back loop of next dc, 3ch, 1dc into centre ring, miss next dc) 4 times, ss into first ch. Fasten off.
Place 4 petal flower on top of 5 petal flower and attach both to garment using photograph as guide.

Using yarn B, make a French knot (by wrapping yarn 3 times round needle) in centre of each flower.
Ties (make 2)
Using 4.00mm (USA G6) hook and yarn B, make a chain 30cm long. Fasten off.
Attach one to each neck edge.

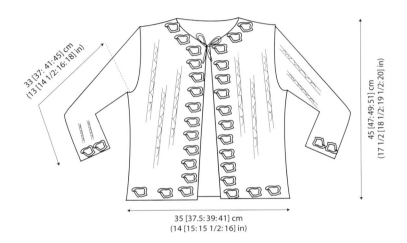

33 [37: 41:45] cm
(13 [14 1/2: 16:18] in)

45 [47:49:51] cm
(17 1/2 [18 1/2:19 1/2:20] in)

35 [37.5: 39: 41] cm
(14 [15: 15 1/2: 16] in)

Nightingale
Marie Wallin

SIZE

	3/4	5/6	7/8	9/10	yrs
To fit chest					
	55–57	59–61	63–67	69–73	cm

YARN

Rowan 4ply Cotton
Yarn A (Navy 150)

	5	5	6	6	x 50g

Yarn B (Steel Blue 149)

	1	1	1	1	x 50g

Yarn C (Fennel 135)

	1	1	1	1	x 50g

Yarn D (Cream 153)

	1	1	1	1	x 50g

Yarn E (Violetta 146)

	1	1	1	1	x 50g

Yarn F (Cheeky 133)

	1	1	1	1	x 50g

NEEDLES

1 pair 3mm (no 11) (USA 3) needles
1 pair 2¾mm (no12) (USA 2)
Stitch holders
2.5 metres of ribbon

TENSION

29 sts and 39 rows to 10cm over st st on 3mm (USA 3)
needles

STRIPE SEQUENCE

Worked in st st throughout
Rows 1 to 6 – Yarn A
Rows 7 to 9 – Yarn B
Rows 10 and 11 – Yarn C
Rows 12 to 21 – Yarn A
Rows 22 to 27 – Yarn D
Rows 28 to 32 – Yarn E
Rows 33 to 50 – Yarn A
Rows 51 to 53 – Yarn C
Rows 54 to 59 – Yarn A
Rows 60 to 62 – Yarn F
Rows 63 to 68 – Yarn A
Rows 69 to 73 – Yarn D
Rows 74 to 84 – Yarn A

BACK

Using 3mm (USA 3) needles and yarn A, cast on
122 128, 134, 140] sts.
Beg with a K row work 12 rows st st, ending with RS
facing for next row.
Work 84 row stripe sequence and rep throughout
shaping sides by dec 1 st at each end of 20th and every
foll 6th row to 104 [110, 116, 122] sts.
Cont straight until back meas 28 [29, 30, 31]cm,
ending with RS facing for next row. *
Shape raglan
Keeping stripe sequence correct dec 1 st at each end of
next 3 [3, 1, 1] rows, then every foll alt row to 48 [50,
54, 56] sts.
Leave rem 48 [50, 54, 56] sts on a stitch holder.

FRONT

Work as given for Back to *.
Shape raglan
Keeping stripe sequence correct dec 1 st at each end
of next 3 [3, 1, 1] rows, then every foll alt row to
58 [60, 64, 66] sts.
Work 1 row, ending with RS facing for next row.
Shape neck
Next row – K2tog, K13, turn and work this side first.
Work 1 row more.
Dec 1 st at raglan edge in next and every foll alt row
at same time dec 1 st at neck edge in every row to 2 sts.
Next row – K2tog. Fasten off.
With RS facing slip centre 28 [30, 34, 36] sts onto a
stitch holder, rejoin yarn to rem sts, K to last 2 sts,
K2tog.
Complete to match first side reversing shapings

SLEEVES (Both alike)

Using 3mm (USA 3) needles and yarn A, cast on
70 [72, 76, 78] sts.
Beg with a K row work 12 rows in st st, ending with
RS facing for next row.
Work 84 row stripe sequence and repeat throughout
shaping sides by inc 1 st at each end of 15th and every
foll 16th [18th, 20th, 24th] row to 84 [86, 90, 92] sts.
Cont straight until sleeve meas 36 [40, 44, 48]cm,
ending with RS facing for next row.
Shape raglan
Keeping stripe sequence correct dec 1 st at each end of

next 19 [17, 17, 15] rows, then every foll alt row to 12 sts. Leave rem 12 sts on a stitch holder.

MAKING UP

Join raglan seams leaving left back seam open.

Neck edging

With RS facing, using 2¾mm (USA 2) needles and yarn A, Knit across 12 sts left on a stitch holder at top of left sleeve, pick up and knit 6 sts down left side of neck, knit across 28 [30, 34, 36] sts left on a stitch holder at front of neck, pick up and knit 6 sts up right side of neck, knit across 12 sts left on a stitch holder at top of right sleeve and knit across 48 [50, 54, 56] sts left on a stitch holder at back of neck.
112 [116, 124, 128] sts.
Knit 2 rows. Cast off.
Join left raglan seam.
Join side and sleeve seams.

Bottom and sleeve edging

Turn back first 12 rows of st st and slip st to inside to form casings.
Thread ribbons through casings.

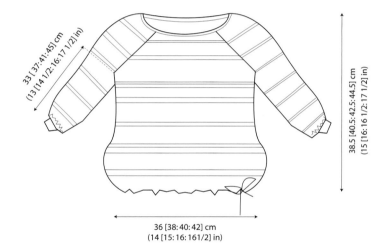

33 [37:41:45] cm
(13 [14 1/2:16:17 1/2] in)

38.5 [40.5:42.5:44.5] cm
(15 [16:16 1/2:17 1/2] in)

36 [38: 40: 42] cm
(14 [15: 16: 161/2] in)

Magpie
Marie Wallin

SIZE

	3/4	5/6	7/8	9/10	yrs

To fit chest

55–57	59–61	63–67	69–73	cm

YARN

Rowan Denim
Yarn A (Memphis 229)

9	10	11	11	x 50g

Yarn B (Nashville 225)

1	1	1	1	x 50g

NEEDLES

1 pair 4mm (no 8) (USA 6) needles

TENSION

25 sts and 28 rows to 10cm over rib on 4mm (USA 6) needles (21sts and 30 rows after finishing)

BACK

Using 4mm (USA 6) needles and yarn A, cast on 86 [92, 98, 104] sts.
Row 1 (RS) – K6, * P2, K4, rep from * to last 8 sts, P2, K6.
Row 2 – P6, * K2, P4, rep from * to last 8 sts, K2, P6.
These 2 rows form rib.
Cont in rib until back meas 28.5 [30, 31.5, 33]cm, ending with RS facing for next row.
Now set sts for raglan patt:-
Row 1(RS) – P8 * K4, P2, rep from* to last 12 sts, K4, P8.
Row 2 – P12, * K2, P4, rep from * to last 14 sts, K2, P12.
Row 3 – K2, P6, * K4, P2, rep from * to last 12 sts, K4, P6, K2.
Row 4 – As row 2.
Row 5 – K4, P6, K2, P2, * K4, P2, rep from * to last 12 sts, K2, P6, K4.
Row 6 – As row 2.
Row 7 – K6, P6, rib to last 12 sts, P6, K6.
Row 8 – P12, rib to last 12 sts, P12.
Rows 7 and 8 form raglan patt.
Shape raglan
Row 1– Sl 1, K1, psso, K5, P6, rib to last 13 sts, P6, K5, K2tog.

Row 2 – P2tog, P11, rib to last 13 sts, P11, P2togtbl. 86 [88, 94, 100] sts. **
Cont in raglan patt dec 1 st at each end as before in next 7 [9, 11, 13] rows, then every foll alt row to 28 [30, 32, 34] sts.
Work 1 row. Cast off.

FRONT

Work as given for Back to **.
Cont in raglan patt dec 1 st at each end as before in next 7 [9, 11, 13] rows, then every foll alt row to 46 [48, 50, 52] sts.
Work 1 row.

Divide for neck
Next row – Sl 1, K1, psso, patt 15, turn and work this side first.
Work 1 row more.
Dec 1 st at each end of next and every foll alt row to 2 sts.
Next row – P2tog. Fasten off.
With RS facing rejoin yarn to rem sts, cast off centre 10 [12, 14, 16] sts, patt to last 2 sts, K2tog.
Complete to match first side.

SLEEVES

Using 4mm (USA 6) needles and yarn A, cast on 46 [48, 50, 52] sts.
Row 1 – (RS) K0 [0, 0, 1], P0 [1, 2, 2], * K4, P2, rep from * to last 4 [5, 0, 1] sts, K4 [4, 0, 1], P0 [1, 0, 0].
Row 2 – P0 [0, 0, 1], K0 [1, 2, 2], * P4, K2, rep from * to last 4 [5, 0, 1] sts, P4 [4, 0, 1], K0 [1, 0, 0] .
These 2 rows form rib.
Cont in rib shaping sides by inc 1 st at each end of 3rd and every foll 8th [8th, 10th, 10th] row to 66 [58, 68, 60] sts, then every foll 10th [10th, 12th, 12th] row to 68 [70, 72, 74] sts,
working inc sts in rib.
Cont straight until sleeve meas 33 [37, 42, 46]cm, ending with RS facing for next row.
Now set sts for raglan patt by working the 8 rows as given for back.
Rows 7 and 8 form raglan patt.
Shape raglan
Keeping raglan patt correct and working decs as given

for back, dec 1 st at each end of next 7 [5, 3, 1] rows, then on every foll alt row to 18 sts. Cast off.

MAKING UP
Join raglan seams. Join side and sleeve seams.
Neckband
Using 4mm (USA 6) needles and yarn A cast on 88 [94, 100, 106] sts.
Row 1 – (RS) * K4, P2, rep from * to last 4 sts, K4.

Row 2 - * P4, K2, rep from * to last 4 sts, P4.
These 2 rows form rib.
Cont in rib until neckband meas 3cm, ending with RS facing for next row. Cast off.
Sew cast on edge of neckband to neck edge leaving row end edges open at centre front.
Edge stitching.
Using yarn B double, oversew raglan seams using photograph as a guide.

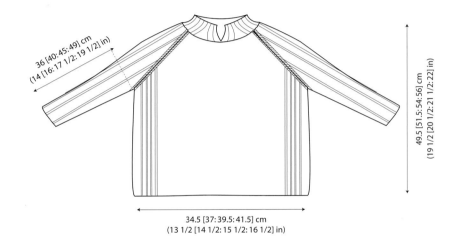

36 [40:45:49] cm
(14 [16:17 1/2:19 1/2] in)

49.5 [51.5:54:56] cm
(19 1/2 [20 1/2:21 1/2: 22] in)

34.5 [37: 39.5: 41.5] cm
(13 1/2 [14 1/2: 15 1/2: 16 1/2] in)

Curlew
Marie Wallin

SIZE

3/4	5/6	7/8	9/10	yrs

To fit chest
55–57   59–61   63–67   69–73cm

YARN
Rowan Cotton Glace (Heather 828)

8	9	10	11	x 50g

NEEDLES
1 pair 3¼mm (no 10) (USA 3) needles
1 3.00mm (no 1) (USA C2) crochet hook

TENSION
25 sts and 34 rows to 10cm over st st on 3¼mm
(USA 3) needles

CROCHET ABBREVIATIONS
ch = chain; ss = slip stitch; dc = double crochet;
tr = treble crochet; ch sp = chain space.

LEFT FRONT
Using 3¼mm (USA3) needles cast on 44 [46, 49, 51] sts.
Beg with a K row, work 2 [10, 16, 20] rows in st st. **
Next row – K4 [1, 4, 1], *yfwd, sl1, K1, psso, K3, rep
from * to end.
Beg with a P row, work 3 rows more in st st.
Shape neck
Dec 1 st at end of next and every foll 4th row to 35 [38,
42, 44] sts.
Work 3 rows straight ending with RS facing for next row.
Shape armhole
Next row – Cast off 7 [6, 4, 3] sts, K to last 2 sts, K2tog.
27 [31, 37, 40] sts.
Next row – Purl.
Dec 1 st at armhole edge in next 3 rows then 2 foll alt
rows at same time dec 1 st at neck edge in 3rd and every
foll 4th row to 18 [21, 19, 21] sts.

Sizes 3/4 and 5/6 yrs only
Dec 1 st at neck edge only in every foll 6th row to
14 [16, -, -] sts.

All sizes
Cont straight until armhole meas 15.5 [16.5,

17.5, 18.5]cm, ending with RS facing for next row
Shape shoulder
Next row – Cast off 7 [8, 9, 10] sts, K to end.
Work 1 row more.
Cast off rem 7 [8, 10, 11] sts.

RIGHT FRONT
Work as given for Left front to **.
Next row – K3, yfwd, sl1, K1, psso, rep from * to last 4
[1, 4, 1] sts, K4 [1, 4, 1].
Complete to match Left front reversing shapings and
working 1 row more before armhole and shoulder
shaping.

BACK
Using 3¼mm (USA 3) needles cast on 88 [92, 98, 102] sts.
Beg with a K row work 2 [10, 16, 20] rows in st st..
Next row – K1 [2, 2, 3], * yfwd, Sl1, K1, psso, K3,
rep from * to last 2 [4, 2, 4] sts, yfwd,sl1, K1, psso,
K0 [2, 0, 2].
Beg with a P row cont in st st until back matches Fronts
to armhole shaping, ending with RS facing for next row.
Shape armholes
Cast off 7 [6, 4, 3] sts at beg of next 2 rows.
74 [80, 90, 96] sts.
Dec 1 st at each end of next 3 rows, then 2 foll alt rows.
64 [70, 80, 86] sts.
Cont straight until back matches Fronts to shoulder
shaping, ending with RS facing for next row.
Shape back neck and shoulders
Next row – Cast off 7 [8, 9, 10] sts, K until there are
8 [9, 11, 12] sts on right hand needle, turn and work this
side first.
Next row – P2tog, P to end.
Cast off rem 7 [8, 10, 11] sts.
With RS facing rejoin yarn to rem sts, cast off centre
34 [36, 40, 42] sts, K to end.
Complete to match first side reversing shapings.

SLEEVES (Both alike)
Using 3¼mm (USA 3) needles cast on 62 [64, 66, 68] sts.
Beg with a K row cont in st st shaping sides by dec
1 st at each end of 9th [11th, 13th, 15th] and every foll
6th [8th, 8th, 8th] row to 54 [56, 58, 60] sts.
Work 7 [9, 11, 13] rows straight.
Inc 1 st at each end of next and every foll 4th [4th, 4th,

6th] row to 78 [76, 68, 84] sts.
Sizes 5/6 and 7/8 yrs only
Inc 1 st at each end of foll 6th row to – [80, 82, -] sts.

All sizes
Cont straight until sleeve meas 25 [29, 33, 37]cm, ending with RS facing for next row.
Shape top
Cast off 7 [6, 4, 3] sts at beg of next 2 rows.
64 [68, 74, 78] sts.
Dec 1 st at each end of next 4 rows. 56 [60, 66, 70] sts.
Cast off 2 [3, 5, 6] sts at beg of next 2 rows and 3 [4, 5, 6] sts at beg of foll 2 rows.
Cast off rem 46 sts.

MAKING UP
Join side and shoulder seams.
Welt edging
With RS facing using 3.00mm (USA C2) crochet hook beg at bottom edge of left front:-
Base row – 1ch, 1dc into each st to end, turn.
Next row – 1ch, 1dc into each dc to end ensuring you have a multiple of 3 sts plus 2.
Row 1 – (RS) 1ch, 1dc into 2nd dc, 1dc into next dc, * 4ch, ss into 4th ch from hook, (1picot made), 1dc into each of next 3dc, rep from * to end omitting 1dc at end of last rep, turn.
Row 2- 5ch, miss 2dc, 1tr into next dc, * 2ch, miss 2dc, 1tr into next dc, rep from * to end, turn.
Row 3 – 1ch, 1dc into 1st tr, * (1dc, 1picot, 1dc) into next 2 ch sp, 1dc into next tr, rep from * to end, working last dc into 3rd of 5ch at beg of previous row, turn.
Rep rows 2 and 3 three times more then row 2 once more.
Row 11 – 1ch, 1dc into 1st tr, * 2dc into 2 ch sp, 1dc into next tr, rep from * to 5ch loop, 1dc into loop, 1dc into 3rd ch of loop, turn.
Row 12 – 1ch, 1dc into each dc to end. Fasten off.
Sleeve edging (Both alike)
Work as given for Welt edging.
Join sleeve seams. Insert sleeves.
Circle motifs (Make 12 [13, 14, 15])
Using 3.00mm (USA C2) crochet hook make 8ch, ss into 1st ch to form a ring.

Round 1 – 3ch, work 15tr into ring, ss into 3rd of 3ch at beg of round.
Round 2 – 5ch, (1tr into next tr, 2ch) 15 times, ss into 3rd of 5ch at beg of round.
Round 3 – 1ch, work 3dc into each of 16 2ch sps, ss into 1st dc, Fasten off.
Attach circles evenly around base of garment, securing together at same time.
Scallop edging
With RS facing using 3.00mm (USA C2) crochet hook, beg at bottom edge of right front and proceed as follows:-
Row 1 – 1ch, * 1dc into next 2 sts, 2dc into ch sp, rep from * to start of knitting, 1dc into alternate st until start of crochet edge on left front, * 1dc into next 2 sts, 2dc into each ch sp, rep from * to end, turn.
Row 2 – 1ch, 1dc into each dc to end, turn.
Row 3 – (RS) 1dc into 1st dc, * miss 1dc, 5tr into next dc, miss 1dc, 1dc into next dc, rep from * to end. Fasten off.
Tie
Using 3.00mm (USA C2) crochet hook make a chain 110cm long.
Thread through eyelet holes.

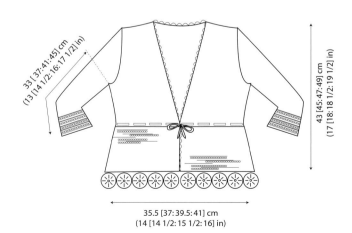

33 [37:41:45] cm (13 [14 1/2:16:17 1/2] in)

43 [45:47:49] cm (17 [18:18 1/2:19 1/2] in)

35.5 [37:39.5:41] cm (14 [14 1/2:15 1/2:16] in)

Pipit
Marie Wallin

Pipit (left)

SIZE

3/4	5/6	7/8	9/10	yrs

To fit chest

55–57	59–61	63–67	69–73	cm

YARN

Rowan Cotton Glace
Yarn A (Candy Floss 747)

6	7	8	8	x 50g

Yarn B (Oyster 730)

1	1	2	2	x 50g

NEEDLES

1 pair 3¼mm (no 10) (USA 3) needles
1 3.00mm (no 1) (USA C2) crochet hook

TENSION

25 sts and 34 rows to 10cm over st st on 3¼mm
(USA 3) needles

CROCHET ABBREVIATIONS

ch = chain; dc = double crochet; tr = treble crochet;
yo = yarn over; ch sp = chain space

BACK

Using 3¼mm (USA 3) needles and yarn A, cast on
80 [86, 90, 94] sts.
Beg with a K row cont in st st until back meas 17 [18,
19, 20]cm, ending with RS facing for next row.
Shape armholes
Cast off 5 [5, 3, 2] sts at beg of next 2 rows.
70 [76, 84, 90] sts.
Dec 1 st at each end of next 3 rows, then 3 foll alt
rows. 58 [64, 72, 78] sts.
Cont straight until armhole meas 14.5 [15.5,
16.5, 17.5]cm, ending with RS facing for next row.
Shape back neck and shoulders
Next row – K17 [19, 20, 24], turn and work this side
first.
Next row – Cast off 3 sts, P to end. 14 [16, 19, 21] sts.
Work 1 row more.
Dec 1 st at beg of next row. 13 [15, 18, 20] sts.
Next row – Cast off 5 [6, 8, 9] sts, K to last 2 sts,
K2tog. 7 [8, 9, 10] sts.
Dec 1 st at beg of next row.
Cast off rem 6 [7, 8, 9] sts.

With RS facing rejoin yarn to rem sts, cast off centre
24 [26, 28, 30] sts, K to end.
Complete to match first side reversing shapings.

LEFT FRONT

Using 3¼mm (USA 3) needles and yarn A, cast on
28 [30, 31, 32] sts.
Beg with a K row cont in st st until left front meas
17 [18, 19, 20]cm, ending with RS facing for next row.
Shape armhole
Next row – Cast off 5 [5, 3, 2] sts, K to end.
23 [25, 28, 30] sts.
Work 1 row more.
Dec 1 st at armhole edge (beg) in next 3 rows, then
3 foll alt rows. 17 [19, 22, 24] sts.
Cont straight until left front matches Back to back
neck and shoulder shaping, ending with RS facing for
next row.
Work 1 row more.
Shape front neck and shoulder
Next row – Cast of 3 sts, P to end. 14 [16, 19, 21] sts.
Work 1 row more.
Dec 1 st at beg of next row. 13 [15, 18, 20] sts.
Next row – Cast off 5 [6, 8, 9] sts, K to last 2 sts,
K2tog. 7 [8, 9, 10] sts.
Dec 1 st at beg of next row.
Cast off rem 6 [7, 8, 9] sts.

RIGHT FRONT

Work to match Left front reversing shapings, working
1 row more before armhole and shoulder shaping and
1 row less before neck shaping.

SLEEVES (Both alike)

Using 3¼mm (USA 3) needles and yarn A, cast on
42 [46, 48, 50] sts.
Beg with a K row cont in st st shaping sides by inc 1 st
at each end of 5th and every foll 6th [6th, 8th, 8th]
row to 66 [56, 68, 56] sts.

Sizes 5/6, 7/8 and 9/10 yrs only
Inc 1 st at each end of foll – [8th, 10th, 10th] row to
– [70, 72, 74] sts.

All sizes
Cont straight until sleeve meas 26.5 [30.5, 34.5, 38.5]cm,
ending with RS facing for next row.

Shape top

Cast off 5 [5, 3, 2] sts at beg of next 2 rows.
56 [60, 66, 70] sts.
Dec 1 st at each end of next 5 rows, then on 2 foll alt rows. 42 [46, 52, 56] sts.
Work 1 row more.
Cast off 6 [8, 11, 13] sts at beg of next 2 rows.
Cast off rem 30 sts.

MAKING UP

Join side and shoulder seams.

Edging

With RS facing using 3.00mm (USA C2) hook and yarn B, beg at neck edge of left front:-
Row 1 – 1ch, 1dc into every other row down left front to bottom edge, 2dc into corner st, 1dc into each st to end, 2dc into corner st, 1dc into every other row up right front to neck edge. Fasten off.
Row 2- With WS facing using yarn A, 1ch, 1dc into each dc to end, working 3dc into each corner.
Fasten off.
Row 3 – With RS facing using yarn B, rejoin yarn to bottom edge, work 6ch, miss 5ch, 1tr into next dc, * 5ch, miss 5dc,1tr into next dc, rep from * to end of bottom edge, working last tr into corner dc, turn.
Row 4 – 6ch, work 1 bobble (work 3tr into next st until 1 loop of each remains on hook, yo and through all 4 loops on hook) into last tr, 8 into next tr work (1 bobble, 3ch, 1bobble), rep from * to last 6ch space, work 1 bobble, 6ch, 1 dc into1st ch sp, ss, fasten off,

Rep rows 3 and 4 along both front edges beg at neck edge on left front and bottom edge on right front.
Row 5 – With RS facing using yarn A, beg at left front edge ** 2dc into 6ch loop, * 1dcinto top of 1st bobble, 1 dc between 1st and 2nd bobble, 1 dc into top of 2nd bobble, 3dc into 3ch loop, rep from * until end 6ch loop, 2dc into 6 ch loop, 8ch, cont along bottom edge from * then along right front edge from ** to end, 1ch, turn.
Row 6 -1ch, 1dc into each dc to end, working 8dcs into each 8ch sp. Fasten off.
Row 7 – With RS facing using yarn B, 1ch, 1dc into each of 1st 2 dcs, * 1dc inserting hook 2 rows lower, 1dc into each of next 2dcs, rep from * to 8dc loop, 1dc into each of 8 dcs, ** 1dc inserting hook 2 rows lower, 1dc into each of next 2 dcs, rep from ** to end, turn.
Row 8 – 1ch, miss 1dc, * miss 1dc, 5tr into next dc, miss 1dc, 1dc into next dc, rep from * ending 1dc.
Fasten off.

Cuffs

Work as given for Edging.
Join sleeve seams. Insert sleeves.

Neck edging

Work rows 5 to 8 as given for Edging

Ties (make 2)

Using 3.00mm (USA C2) crochet hook and yarn A, make ch 20cm long, turn and work 1dc into 2nd ch from hook, then 1dc into each ch to end, fasten off.
Attach 1 tie at each front neck edge and another set 15cm lower.

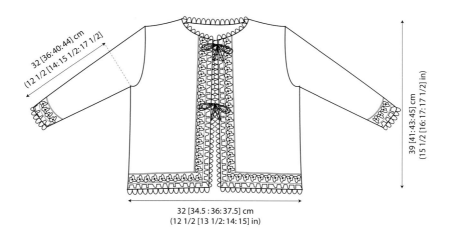

32 [36:40:44] cm
(12 1/2 [14:15 1/2:17 1/2])

39 [41:43:45] cm
(15 1/2 [16:17:17 1/2] in)

32 [34.5 : 36: 37.5] cm
(12 1/2 [13 1/2: 14: 15] in)

Lapwing
Sarah Hatton

Lapwing (right)

SIZE

3/4	5/6	7/8	9/10	yrs

To fit chest

55–57	59–61	63–67	69–73	cm

YARN

Rowan Kidsilk Haze (Mist 636)

4	5	5	6	x 25g

NEEDLES

1 pair 4mm (no 8) (USA 6) needles
1 pair 3mm (no 11) (USA 3) double pointed needles
1 button

TENSION

22 sts and 32 rows to 10cm over st st (with 2 ends of yarn) and 22 sts and 31 rows over patt (with 1 end of yarn) on 4mm (USA 6) needles

BACK

Using 4mm (USA 6) needles and a single end of yarn, cast on 91 [97, 103, 109] sts, loosely.
Purl 3 rows, ending with RS facing for next row.
Rep 10 rows of patt foll chart dec 1 st at each end of 11th and every foll 4th row to 67 [71, 75, 81] sts.
Work 11 rows straight.
Inc 1 st at each end of next and 3 foll 4th rows, working inc sts in patt. 75 [79, 83, 89] sts.

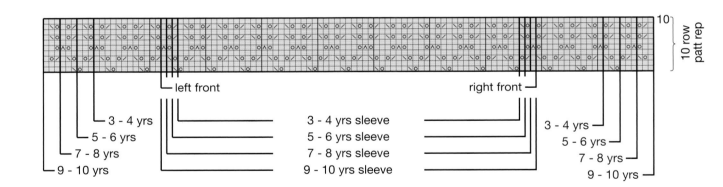

Key

▣ K on RS,
P on WS

◉ yfwd

☑ K2tog

◩ sl 1, K1, psso

◪ sl 1, K2tog, psso

Work 1 row more, ending with RS facing for next row.

Join in second strand of yarn

Beg with a K row cont in st st inc 1 st at each end of 3rd row. 77 [81, 85, 91] sts.

Cont straight until back meas 30.5 [31.5, 33, 33]cm, ending with RS facing for next row.

Shape armholes

Cast off 4 [3, 2, 2] sts at beg of next 2 rows. 69 [75, 81, 87] sts.

Dec 1 st at each end of next 3 rows, then 3 foll alt rows. 57 [65, 69, 75] sts.

Cont straight until armhole meas 15.5 [16.5, 17.5, 18.5]cm, ending with RS facing for next row.

Shape shoulders

Next row – Cast off 5 [6, 7, 8] sts, K until there are 7 [8, 9, 10] sts on right hand needle, turn and work this side first.

Next row – P2tog, P to end.

Cast off rem 6 [7, 8, 9] sts.

With RS facing rejoin 2 ends of yarn to rem sts, cast off centre 33 [35, 37, 39] sts, K to end.

Complete to match first side reversing shapings.

LEFT FRONT

Using 4mm (USA 6) needles and a single end of yarn, cast on 79 [82, 85, 88] sts.

Purl 3 rows, ending with RS facing for next row.

Rep 10 rows of patt as given foll chart dec 1 st at side edge (beg) in 11th and every foll 4th row to 67 [69, 71, 74] sts.

Work 11 rows straight.

Inc 1 st at side edge in next and 3 foll 4th rows, working inc sts in patt. 71 [73, 75, 78] sts.

Work 1 row more.

Join in second strand of yarn

Beg with a K row cont in st st, work 1 row more, ending with WS facing for next row.

Shape neck

Inc 1 st at side edge of 2nd row **at same time** cast off 4 sts at neck edge (beg) in next and 2 foll alt rows, then 3 sts on 3 foll alt rows. 51 [53, 55, 58] sts.

Shape armhole

Next row – Cast off 4 [3, 2, 2] sts, K to last 2 sts, K2tog. 46 [49, 52, 55] sts.

Next row - P2tog, P to end. 45 [48, 51, 54] sts.

Dec 1 st at armhole edge in next 3 rows, then 3 foll alt rows **at same time** dec 1 st at neck edge in every row. 30 [33, 36, 39] sts.

Work 1 row, ending with RS facing for next row.

Dec 1 st at neck edge only in next and every foll alt row to 11 [13, 15, 17] sts.

Cont straight until front matches Back to shoulder shaping, ending with RS facing for next row.

Shape shoulder

Next row – Cast off 5 [6, 7, 8] sts, K to end.

Work 1 row more.

Cast off rem 6 [7, 8, 9] sts.

RIGHT FRONT

Work to match Left front reversing shapings, working 1 row more before shoulder shaping and 1 row less before neck shaping.

SLEEVES (Both alike)

Using 4mm (USA 6) needles and a single end of yarn, cast on 61 [63, 65, 67] sts.

Purl 3 rows, ending with RS facing for next row.

Work 10 rows of patt from chart.

Cont rep rows 9 and 10 only shaping sides by inc 1 st at each end of 7th row then foll 20th row. 65 [67, 69, 71] sts.

Cont straight until sleeve meas 32 [36, 40, 44]cm, ending with RS facing for next row.

Shape top

Keeping patt correct, cast off 4 [3, 2, 2] sts at beg of next 2 rows. 57 [61, 65, 67] sts.

Dec 1 st at each end of next 8 rows. 41 [45, 49, 51] sts.

Cast off 5 [6, 7, 8] sts at beg of next 2 rows. 31 [33, 35, 35] sts.

Cast off 5 [6, 7, 7] sts at beg of next 2 rows.

Cast off rem 21 sts.

MAKING UP

Join side and shoulder seams. Insert sleeves.

Neck edging and ties

Using 3.00mm (USA 3) double pointed needles cast on 4 sts.

Row 1 – K4, * without turning slip these 4 sts to

opposite end of needle and bring yarn to opposite end of work pulling it tightly across WS of work, K these 4 sts again, rep from * until tie is long enough to go around left side of neck across back neck and down right side of neck, leaving 25 cm loose at right side.

Slip stitch tie in place.
Make a 2nd tie 25cm long and attach to left side seam to correspond.
Sew button to inside of right side seam and use a natural hole in lace pattern to fasten.

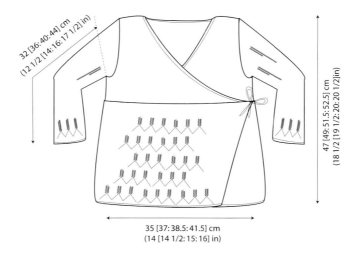

32 [36:40:44] cm
(12 1/2 [14:16:17 1/2] in)

47 [49:51.5:52.5] cm
(18 1/2 [19 1/2:20:20 1/2]in)

35 [37:38.5:41.5] cm
(14 [14 1/2:15:16] in)

Linnet

Marie Wallin

SIZE

	3/4	5/6	7/8	9/10	yrs
To fit chest					
	55–57	59–61	63–67	69–73	cm

YARN

Rowan Kidsilk Haze
Yarn A (Trance 582)

	1	1	1	1	x 25g

Yarn B (Glacier 640)

	2	2	2	2	x 25g

NEEDLES

1 pair 3¼mm (no 10) (USA 3) needles
Stitch holders

TENSION

25 sts and 34 rows to 10cm over st st on 3¼mm
(USA 3) needles

BACK

Using 3¼mm (USA 3) needles and yarn A, cast on
96 [102, 106, 112] sts.
Beg with a K row work 14 rows in st st, ending with
RS facing for next row.
Next row – (RS) K2, * yfwd, K2tog, rep from * to last
2 sts, K2 (folding row).
Work 13 rows straight, ending with RS facing for next
row. **
Change to yarn B.
Cont in st st shaping sides by dec 1 st at each end of
15th row, then 2 foll 10th [12th, 14th, 16th] rows.
90 [96, 100, 106] sts.
Cont straight until back meas 26 [27, 28, 29] cm from
folding row, ending with RS facing for next row.
Shape armholes
Cast off 5 [5, 3, 3] sts at beg of next 2 rows.
80 [86, 94, 100] sts.
Dec 1 st at each end of next 3 rows, then foll 2 alt
rows. 70 [76, 84, 90] sts.
Cont straight until armhole meas 16.5 [17.5,
18.5, 19.5]cm, ending with RS facing for next row.
Shape back neck and shoulders
Next row – K21 [23, 26, 27] turn and work this side
first.

Next row – Cast off 4 sts, P to end. 17 [19, 22, 23] sts.
Next row – Cast off 8 [9, 10, 11] sts, K to end.
9 [10, 12, 12] sts.
Next row – P2tog, P to end.
Cast off rem 8 [9, 11, 11] sts.
With RS facing, cast off centre 28 [30, 32, 36] sts,
K to end.
Complete to match first side reversing shapings.

FRONT

Work as given for back to **.
Change to yarn B.
Beg with a K row, work 2 rows in st st, ending with RS
facing for next row.
Left side panel
Next row – K29 [31, 32, 33], turn and work this side
first, leaving rem sts on a stitch holder.
Work 11 rows straight.
Dec 1 st at beg of next and 2 foll 10th [12th,
14th, 16th] rows. 26 [28, 29, 30] sts.
Cont straight until left side panel matches Back to
armhole shaping, ending with RS facing for next row.
Shape armhole
Next row - Cast off 5 [5, 3, 3] sts, K to end.
21 [23, 26, 27] sts.
Work 1 row more.
Dec 1 st at armhole edge in next 3 rows, then 2 foll alt
rows. 16 [18, 21, 22] sts.
Cont straight left side panel matches Back to shoulder
shaping, ending with RS facing for next row.
Shape shoulder
Next row - Cast off 8 [9, 10, 11] sts, K to end.
Work 1 row more.
Cast off rem 8 [9, 11, 11] sts.
Centre panel
With RS facing rejoin yarn to rem sts, K38 [40, 42, 46],
turn and work this section first, leaving rem sts on a
stitch holder.
Cont straight until 22 rows less have been worked
than on Back to shoulder shaping, ending with RS
facing for next row. Cast off.
Right side panel
With RS facing rejoin yarn to rem sts, K to end.
Complete to match Left side panel reversing shapings
and working 1 row more before armhole and shoulder
shaping.

MAKING UP

Ties (make 2)

Using 3¼mm (USA 3) needles and yarn A, cast on 12 sts.
Beg with a K row, cont in st st until tie meas 22cm,
ending with RS facing for next row.
Dec 1 st at each end of next and every foll alt row to
2 sts, P2tog. Fasten off.
Join front side panels to centre panel inserting ties
28cm down from shoulder.
Turn back welt and slip stitch in place 1 row below
colour change.
Join right shoulder seam.

Neck edging

With RS facing using 3¼mm (USA 3) needles and yarn
A, pick up and knit 19 sts down left side of neck,
32 [34, 36, 40] sts from front neck, 19 sts up right side
of neck, 5 sts down side of back neck, 24 [26, 28, 32] sts
from back neck and 5 sts up side of back neck.
104 [108, 112, 120] sts.
Next row – Knit.
Next row – Cast off 2 sts, * slip st on right hand
needle back onto left hand needle, cast on 2 sts, cast
off 4 sts, rep from * to end.
Join left shoulder seam.

Armhole edging (both alike)

With RS facing using 3¼mm (USA 3) needles and yarn
A, pick up and knit 98 [104, 110, 114] sts evenly
around armhole edge.
Work as given for Neck edging.
Join side seams.

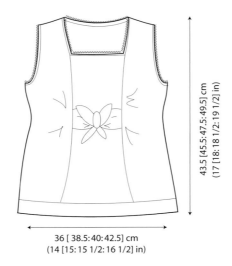

43.5 [45.5:47.5:49.5] cm
(17 [18:18 1/2:19 1/2] in)

36 [38.5: 40: 42.5] cm
(14 [15: 15 1/2: 16 1/2] in)

Swift

Marie Wallin

SIZE

	3/4	5/6	7/8	9/10	yrs

To fit chest

	55–57	59–61	63–67	69–73	cm

YARN

Rowan Handknit Cotton
Yarn A (Delphinium 334)

	5	6	6	7	x 50g

Yarn B (Antique 333)

	4	4	5	5	x 50g

NEEDLES

1 pair 6mm (no 4) (USA 10) needles
1 pair 4mm (no 8) (USA 6) needles
1 pair 3¼mm (no 10) (USA 3) needles
1 x 4.00mm (no 8) (USA G6) crochet hook
1 metre of velvet ribbon

TENSION

20 sts and 28 rows to 10cm over st st on 4mm (USA 6) needles

CROCHET ABBREVIATIONS

ch = chain; dc = double crochet; tr = treble crochet; ss = slip stitch.

BACK

Using 6mm (USA 10) needles and yarn A double, cast on 71 [75, 79, 83] sts.
Knit 18 rows.
Change to 4mm (USA 6) needles
Using yarn A single, beg with a K row work 2 rows in st st.
Change to yarn B and cont in st st until back meas 24 [25, 26, 27]cm, ending with RS facing for next row.
Shape armholes
Cast off 6 [5, 4, 3] sts at beg of next 2 rows.
59 [65, 71, 77] sts.
Dec 1 st at each end of next and 3 foll alt rows.
51 [57, 63, 69] sts.
Cont straight until armhole meas 15.5 [16.5, 17.5, 18.5]cm, ending with RS facing for next row.
Shape shoulders
Next row – Cast off 5 [6, 7, 8] sts, K until there are

9 [10, 11, 12] sts on right hand needle, turn and work this side first.
Next row – Cast off 3 sts, P to end.
Cast off rem 6 [7, 8, 9] sts.
With RS facing rejoin yarn to rem sts, cast off centre 23 [25, 27, 29] sts, K to end.
Complete to match first side reversing shapings.

LEFT FRONT

Using 6mm (USA 10) needles and yarn A double, cast on 35 [37, 39, 41] sts.
Knit 18 rows.
Change to 4mm (USA 6) needles
Using yarn A single, beg with a K row work 2 rows in st st.
Change to yarn B and cont in st st until left front matches Back to armhole shaping, ending with RS facing for next row.
Shape armhole
Next row – Cast off 6 [5, 4, 3] sts, K to end.
29 [32, 35, 38] sts.
Work 1 row more.
Dec 1 st at beg of next and 3 foll alt rows.
25 [28, 31, 34] sts.
Cont straight until 13 rows less have been worked than on Back to shoulder shaping, ending with WS facing for next row.
Shape neck
Next row – Cast off 7 [8, 9, 10] sts, P to end.
18 [20, 22, 24] sts.
Dec 1 st at neck edge in next 7 rows. 11 [13, 15, 17] sts.
Cont straight until Left front matches Back to shoulder shaping, ending with RS facing for next row.
Shape shoulder
Next row – Cast off 5 [6, 7, 8] sts, K to end.
Work 1 row more.
Cast off rem 6 [7, 8, 9] sts.

RIGHT FRONT

Work to match Left front reversing shapings, working 1 row more before armhole and shoulder shaping and 1 row less before neck shaping.

SLEEVES (Both alike)

Using 6mm (USA 10) needles and yarn A double, cast on 34 [36, 38, 40] sts.

Knit 18 rows.

Change to 4mm (USA 6) needles

Using yarn A single beg with a K row work 2 rows in st st.

Change to yarn B and cont in st st shaping sides by inc 1 st at each end of 5th and every foll 6th [6th, 8th, 8th] row to 52 [46, 58, 50] sts.

Size 5/6 and 9/10 yrs only

Inc 1 st at each end of foll – [8th, - 10th] row to – [56, –, 60] sts.

All sizes

Cont straight until sleeve meas 33 [37, 41, 45]cm, ending with RS facing for next row.

Shape top

Cast off 6 [5, 4, 3] sts at beg of next 2 rows.

40 [46, 50, 54] sts.

Dec 1 st at each end of next and 3 foll alt rows.

32 [38, 42 46] sts.

Work 1 row.

Cast off 5 [6, 7, 8] sts at beg of next 4 rows.

Cast off rem 12 [14, 14, 14] sts.

MAKING UP

Join side, shoulder and sleeve seams.

Insert sleeves.

Front edging (both alike)

With RS facing using 3¼mm (USA 3) needles and yarn B, pick up and knit 66 [70, 74, 78] sts up front edge section worked in yarn B.

Cast off knitways on WS.

Neck edging

Using 4mm (USA G6) crochet hook and yarn A, work dcs around neck edging ensuring that there are a multiple of 4 plus 1dc, turn.

Row 1 – Work 1dc in 1st st, * miss 1dc, 5tr into next dc, miss 1dc, 1dc, rep from * to end. Fasten off.

Circles(make 6)

Using 4mm (USA G6) crochet hook and yarn A work 5ch, ss to 1st dc to form ring.

Round 1 – 3ch, 15tr into ring, ss in 3rd of 3ch at beg of round. Fasten off.

Attach circles using photograph as a guide.

Ties

Thread velvet ribbon through centre of each circle.

33 [37:41:45] cm
(13 [14 1/2:16:17 1/2] in)

41 [43:45:47] cm
(16 [17:17 1/2:18 1/2] in)

35.5 [37.5:39.5:41.5] cm
(14 [15:15 1/2:16] in)

Dove
Marie Wallin

SIZE

	3/4	5/6	7/8	9/10	yrs

To fit chest

55–57	59–61	63–67	69–73	cm

YARN

Rowan Kidsilk Haze
Yarn A (Cream 634)

3	3	3	4	x 25g

Yarn B (Ice Cream 637)

1	1	1	2	x 25g

NEEDLES

1 pair 3¼mm (no 10) (USA 3) needles
1 3.00mm (no 1) (USA C2) crochet hook
4 x 00417 buttons

TENSION

25 sts and 34 rows to 10cm over st st on 3¼mm
(USA 3) needles

CROCHET ABBREVIATIONS

ch = chain; dc = double crochet; tr = treble crochet;

BACK

Using 3¼mm (USA 3) needles and yarn A, cast on
121 [121, 131, 141] sts.
Beg with a K row work 34 [34, 48, 40] rows in st st,
ending with RS facing for next row.
** Change to yarn B.
Pattern panel
Row 1- (RS) K1, * yfwd, K3, Sl1, K2tog, psso, K3,
yfwd, K1, rep from * to end.
Row 2 – Purl.
Row 3 – P1, * K1, yfwd, K2, Sl1, K2tog, psso, K2,
yfwd, K1, P1, rep from * to end.
Row 4 – K1, * P9, K1, rep from * to end.
Row 5 –P1, * K2, yfwd, K1, Sl1, K2tog, psso, K1, yfwd,
K2, P1, rep from * to end.
Row 6 – As row 4.
Row 7 – P1, * K3, yfwd, Sl1, K2tog, psso, yfwd, K3, P1,
rep from * to end.
Row 8 – Purl.
Change to yarn A ***
Beg with a K row work 24 [26, 28, 30] rows in st st,
ending with RS facing for next row.
Rep from ** to *** once.
Beg with a K row work 22 [24, 26, 28] rows in st st,
ending with RS facing for next row. ****
Next row – K6 [13, 1, 0], * (K2tog) twice, K1 [1, 2, 2],
rep from * to last 5 [13, 4, 9] sts, (K2tog) 0 [0, 2, 4]
times, K5 [13, 0, 1]. 77 [83, 87, 93] sts.
Next row – Purl.
Cont in st st shaping sides by inc 1 st at each end of
7th and 3 foll 6th rows. 85 [91, 95, 101] sts.
Cont straight until Back meas 40 [42, 45, 47] cm,
ending with RS facing for next row.
Shape armholes
Cast off 6 [6, 4, 4] sts at beg of next 2 rows.
73 [79, 87, 93] sts.
Dec1 st at each end of next 3 rows, then on 2 foll alt
rows. 63 [69, 77, 83] sts.
Cont straight until armhole meas 15.5 [16.5,
17.5, 18.5]cm, ending with RS facing for next row.
Shape shoulders
Cast off 4 [5, 6, 6] sts at beg of next 2 rows.
55 [59, 65, 71] sts.
Next row – Cast off 4 [5, 6, 7] sts, K until there are
9 [9, 10, 11] sts on right hand needle, turn and work
this side first.
Next row – Cast off 4 sts, P to end.
Cast off rem 5 [5, 6, 7] sts.
With RS facing rejoin yarn to rem sts, cast off centre
29 [31, 33, 35] sts, K to end.
Complete to match first side reversing shapings.

LEFT FRONT

Using 3¼mm (USA 3) needles and yarn A, cast on
51 [51, 61, 71] sts.
Work as give for Back to ****.
Next row – K5 [4, 2, 3], * (K2tog) 1 [1, 1, 2] times,
K1 [2, 1, 1], rep from * to last 4 [3, 2, 3] sts, K4 [3,
2, 3]. 37 [40, 42, 45] sts.

Next row – Purl.

Cont in st st shaping sides by inc 1 st at side edge (beg) in 7th and 3 foll 6th rows. 41 [44, 46, 49] sts.

Cont straight until left front matches Back to armhole shaping, ending with RS facing for next row.

Shape armhole

Next row – Cast off 6 [6, 4, 4] sts, K to end. 35 [38, 42, 45] sts.

Work 1 row more.

Dec 1 st at armhole edge in next 3 rows, then 2 foll alt rows. 30 [33, 37, 40] sts.

Cont straight until 13 [13, 13, 15] rows less have been worked than on Back to shoulder shaping, ending with WS facing for next row.

Shape neck

Next row – (WS) Cast off 9 [10, 11, 12] sts, P to end. 21 [23, 26, 28] sts.

Dec 1 st at neck edge in next 5 rows then 3 foll alt rows. 13 [15, 18, 20] sts.

Work 1 [1, 1, 3] rows more.

Shape shoulder

Cast off 4 [5, 6, 6] sts at beg of next row and 4 [5, 6, 7] sts at beg of foll alt row.

Work 1 row more.

Cast off rem 5 [5, 6, 7] sts.

RIGHT FRONT

Using 3¼mm needles and yarn A, cast on 51 [51, 61, 71] sts.

Work as given for back to ****.

Next row – K5 [5, 3, 4], * (K2tog) 1 [1, 1, 2] times, K1 [2, 1, 1], rep from * to last 4 [2, 1, 2] sts, K4 [2, 1, 2]. 37 [40, 42, 45] sts.

Next row – Purl.

Complete to match Left front reversing shapings and working 1 row more before armhole and shoulder shaping and 1 row less before neck shaping.

MAKING UP

Join shoulder seams.

Neck edging

Using 3.00 (USA C2) crochet hook and yarn A, beg at left side of neck work 1dc into each st up left side of neck, around back neck and down right side of neck, turn.

Next row – 1ch, 1dc into each dc to end.

Work 2 rows more. Fasten off.

Armhole edgings (Both alike)

Work as given for Neck edging.

Join side seams.

Bottom edging

Using 3¼mm (USA 3) needles and yarn B, cast on 12 sts.

Row 1 – (RS) Sl1, K3, yfwd, k2tog, K2, yfwd, K2tog, yfwd, K2. 13 sts.

Row 2 and every foll alt row – Purl.

Row 3 – Sl1, K2, (yfwd, K2tog) twice, K2, yfwd, K2tog, yfwd, K2. 14 sts.

Row 5 – Sl1, K3, (yfwd, K2tog) twice, K2, yfwd, K2tog, yfwd, K2. 15 sts.

Row 7 – Sl1, K2, (yfwd, K2tog) 3 times, K2, yfwd, K2tog, yfwd, K2. 16 sts.

Row 9 – Sl1, K2, K2tog, yfwd, K2tog, yfwd, K2, K2tog, (yfwd, K2tog) twice, K1. 15 sts.

Row 11 – Sl1, K1, K2tog, yfwd, K2tog, yfwd, K2, K2tog, (yfwd, K2tog) twice, K1. 14 sts.

Row 13 – Sl1, K2, K2tog, yfwd, K2, K2tog, (yfwd, K2tog) twice, K1. 13 sts.

Row 15 – Sl1, K1, K2tog, yfwd, K2, K2tog, (yfwd, K2tog) twice, K1. 12 sts.

Row 16 – Purl.

These 16 rows form patt.

Cont in patt until edging is long enough without stretching to fit around bottom edge, ending after patt row 16 has been worked. Cast off.

Slip stitch straight selvedge of edging along bottom edge.

Waist edging

Using 3.00mm (USA C2) crochet hook and yarn B, working on dec row, proceed as follows:-

Foundation row – 1dc into each st around waist section making sure there are a multiple of 4 plus 3 dcs, turn.

Row 1 – 1ch, 1dc into each dc to end, turn.

Row 2 – 3ch, miss 1dc, 5tr into next dc, miss 1dc, 1dc

into next dc, rep from * to end. Fasten off.
Button band
Work as given for Neck edging.
Mark position of buttons, first to be just below neck edge, last to be just above waist and 2 spaced

evenly between.
Buttonhole band
Work as given for neckband, working 3ch to correspond with button positions on row 2.
Sew on buttons.

68 [73: 76: 81] cm
(27 [29: 30: 32] in)

34 [36.5: 38: 40.5] cm
(13 1/2: 14 1/2: 15: 16] in)

Raven

Sarah Hatton

SIZE

3/4	5/6	7/8	9/10	yrs

To fit chest

| 55–57 | 59–61 | 63–67 | 69–73 | cm |

YARN

Rowan All Seasons Cotton (Jersey 191)

| 8 | 9 | 10 | 11 | x 50g |

NEEDLES

1 pair 5mm (no 6) (USA 8) needles
1 pair 4½mm (no 7) (USA 7) needles
1 x 4½mm (no 7) (USA 7) circular needle
Cable needle
Stitch holders

TENSION

20 sts and 24 rows to 10cm over patt on 5mm (USA 6)
needles

SPECIAL ABBREVIATIONS

CN=cable needle
C4B=slip next 2 sts onto CN and hold at back of work,
K2 then K2 from CN.
C4F=slip next 2 sts onto CN and hold at front of work,
K2 then K2 from CN.

BACK

Using 4½mm (USA 7) needles cast on 65 [69, 73, 77] sts.
Knit 2 rows.
Change to 5mm (USA 8) needles
Next row – (RS) K3 [5, 7, 9], (P2, K3, m1, K4, P2, K5)
twice, P2, K4, m1, K3, P2, K5, P2, K4, m1, K3, P2,
K3 [5, 7, 9]. 69 [73, 77, 81] sts.
Next row – P3 [5, 7, 9], * K2, P8, K2, P5, rep from *
twice, K2, P8, K2, P3 [5, 7, 9].
Row 1 – (RS) K3 [5, 7, 9]. * P2, C4B, C4F, P2, K5, rep
from * twice, P2, C4B, C4F, P2, K3 [5, 7, 9].
Row 2 – P3 [5, 7, 9], * K2, P8, K2, P5, rep from *
twice, K2, P8, K2, P3 [5, 7, 9].
Row 3 – K3 [5, 7, 9], * P2, K8, P2, K5, rep from *

twice, P2, K8, P2, K3 [5, 7, 9].
Row 4 – As row 2.
Row 5 – K3 [5, 7, 9], *P2, C4F, C4B, P2, K5, rep from *
twice, P2, C4F, C4B, P2, K3 [5, 7, 9].
Row 6 – As row 2.
Row 7 – As row 3.
Row 8 – As row 2.
These 8 rows form patt.
Cont in patt until back meas 22 [23, 24, 25]cm, ending
with RS facing for next row.
Shape armholes
Keeping patt correct cast off 4 sts at beg of next 2 rows.
61 [65, 69, 73] sts.
Dec 1 st at each end of next 3 rows, then foll alt row.
53 [57, 61, 65] sts. **
Cont straight until armhole meas 15.5 [16.5,
17.5, 18.5]cm, ending with RS facing for next row.
Shape shoulders
Next row – Cast off 6 [6, 7, 7] sts, patt until there are
9 [10, 10, 11] sts on right hand needle, turn and work
this side first.
Next row - Cast off 3 sts, patt to end.
Cast off rem 6 [7, 7, 8] sts.
With RS facing slip centre 23 [25, 27, 29] sts onto a
stitch holder, rejoin yarn to rem sts and patt to end.
Complete to match first side reversing shapings.

FRONT

Work as given for Back to **.
Cont straight until 18 [18, 18, 20] rows less have been
worked than on Back to shoulder shaping, ending with
RS facing for next row.
Divide for front split
Next row – Patt 24 [26, 28, 30] turn and work this side
first.
Work 10 rows more, ending with WS facing for next
row.
Shape neck
Next row – Cast off 9 [10, 11, 12] sts, patt to end.
15 [16, 17, 18] sts.
Dec 1 st at neck edge in next 3 rows.
12 [13, 14, 15] sts.

Cont straight until front matches Back to shoulder shaping, ending with RS facing for next row.

Shape shoulder

Next row – Cast off 6 [6, 7, 7] sts, patt to end.

Work 1 row more.

Cast off rem 6 [7, 7, 8] sts.

With RS rejoin yarn to rem sts, cast off centre 5 sts, patt to end.

Complete to match first side reversing shapings and working 1 row less before neck shaping and 1 row more before shoulder shaping.

SLEEVES (Both alike)

Using 4½mm (USA 7) needles cast on 38 [42, 42, 46] sts.

Row 1 – (RS) * K2, P2, rep from * to last 2 sts, K2.

Row 2 – P2, * K2, P2 rep from * to end.

These 2 rows form 2x2 rib.

Work 4 rows more in rib.

Change to 5mm (USA 8) needles

Next row – K14 [15, 16, 17], P2, K2, m1 [0, 1, 0], K2 [4, 2, 4], m1 [0, 1, 0], K2, P2, K14 [15, 16, 17]. 40 [42, 44, 46] sts.

Next row – P14 [15, 16, 17], K2, P8, K2, P14 [15, 16, 17].

Row 1 – (RS) K14 [15, 16, 17], P2, C4B, C4F, P2, K14 [15, 16, 17].

Row 2 – P14 [15, 16, 17], K2, P8, K2, P14 [15, 16, 17].

Row 3 – K14 [15, 16, 17], P2, K8, P2, K14 [15, 16, 17].

Row 4 – As row 2.

Row 5 – K14 [15, 16, 17], P2, C4F, C4B, P2, K14 [15, 16, 17].

Row 6 – As row 2.

Row 7 – As row 3.

Row 8 - As row 2.

These 8 rows form patt.

Cont in patt shaping sides by inc 1 st at each end of next and every foll 10th [10th, 12th, 14th] row to 52 [46, 50, 54] sts.

Sizes 5/6, 7/8 and 9/10 yrs only

Inc 1 st at each end of every foll – [12th, 14th, 16th] row to – [54, 56, 58] sts.

All sizes

Cont straight until sleeve meas 32 [36, 40, 44] cm, ending with RS facing for next row.

Shape top

Cast off 4 sts at beg of next 2 rows.

44 [46, 48, 50] sts.

Dec 1 st at each end of next 4 rows.

36 [38, 40, 42] sts.

Cast off 10 [11, 12, 13] sts at beg of next 2 rows.

26 sts.

Cast off rem 16 sts.

MAKING UP

Join shoulder seams.

Hood

With RS facing using 4½mm (USA 7) needles beg and ending at front split, pick up and knit 17 [17, 17, 18]sts up right side of neck, 3 sts down right side of back neck, work across 23 [25, 27, 29] sts left on a stitch holder at back of neck as follows:- K3 [4, 5, 6], (inc in next st, K3) 4 times, inc in next st, K3 [4, 5, 6], pick up and knit 3 sts up left side of back neck and 17 [17, 17, 18]sts down left side of neck.

68 [70, 72, 76] sts.

Beg with a P row, cont in st st until hood meas 21 [22, 23, 24]cm ending with RS facing for next row.

Next row – Cast off 23 [23, 24, 25] sts, K until there are 22 [24, 24, 26] sts on right hand needle, cast off rem 23 [23, 24, 25] sts.

Rejoin yarn to WS of rem 22 [24, 24, 26] sts and work a further 14 [14, 14.5, 14.5]cm, ending with RS facing for next row. Cast off.

Join sides of this 14 [14, 14.5, 14.5]cm section to 23 [23, 24, 25] sts cast off earlier to form hood.

Hood border

With RS facing using 4½mm (USA 7) circular needle pick up and knit 10 sts up right side of front split, 108 [116, 116, 120] sts evenly around hood edge and 10 sts down left side of front split.

128 [136, 136, 140] sts.

Row 1 – (WS) K1, P2, * K2, P2, rep from * to last st, K1.

Row 2 – P1, * K2, P2, re from * to last 3 sts, K2, P1.

These 2 rows form rib.
Work 4 rows more in rib.
Cast off in rib.

Placing right side over left sew rib in place at front neck split.
Join side and sleeve seams. Insert sleeves.

32 [36:40:44] cm
(12 1/2 [14:16:17 1/2] in)

39 [41:43:45] cm
(15 1/2 [16:17:18] in)

34.5 [36.5:38.5:40.5] cm
(13 1/2 [14 1/2:15:16]in)

Kite

Sarah Hatton

SIZE

3/4	5/6	7/8	9/10	yrs

To fit chest

55–57	59–61	63–67	69–73	cm

YARN

Rowan All Seasons Cotton (Ravish 199)

6	6	7	8	x 50g

NEEDLES

1 pair 4mm (no 8) (USA 6) needles
1 pair 4½mm (no 7) (USA 7) needles
Stitch holders
1.2 metre ribbon x 0.5cm – 0.75cm wide

TENSION

18 sts and 25 rows to 10cm over st st on 4½mm
(USA 7) needles

BACK

Using 4½mm (USA 7) needles cast on 69 [73, 77, 79] sts.
Purl 2 rows.
Row 3 – (RS) K7 [1, 3, 4], * yfwd, K2, Sl1, K2tog, psso,
K2, yfwd, K1, rep from * to last 6 [0, 2, 3] sts,
K6 [0, 2, 3].
Rows 4 and 6 – Purl.
Row 5 – K7 [1, 3, 4], * K1, yfwd, K1, Sl1, K2tog, psso,
K1, yfwd, K2, rep from * to last 6 [0, 2, 3] sts, K6 [0,
2, 3].
Row 7 – K7 [1, 3, 4], * K2, yfwd, Sl1, K2tog, psso,
yfwd, K3, rep from * to last 6 [0, 2, 3] sts, K6 [0, 2, 3].
Row 8 – P10 [4, 6, 7], * K1, P7, rep from * to last 11 [5,
7, 0] sts, K1 [1, 1, 0], P10 [4, 6, 0].
Row 9 – Knit.
Last 2 rows set patt.
Cont in patt shaping sides by dec 1 st at each end of
6th and 2 foll 8th rows. 63 [67, 71, 73] sts.
Cont straight until back meas 17.5cm, ending with RS
facing for next row.
Next row - * K2tog, yfwd, rep from * to last st, K1.
Beg with a P row cont in st st until back meas 26 [27,
28, 29]cm, ending with RS facing for next row.
Shape armholes
Cast off 5 [5, 4, 3] sts at beg of next 2 rows.
53 [57, 63, 67] sts.

Dec 1 st at each end of next 3 rows, then foll alt row.
45 [49, 55, 59] sts.
Cont straight until armhole meas 15.5 [16.5,
17.5, 18.5]cm, ending with RS facing for next row.
Shape shoulders
Next row – Cast off 5 [5, 6, 7] sts, K until there are
8 [9, 10, 10] sts on right hand needle, turn and work
this side first.
Next row – Cast off 3 sts, patt to end.
Cast off rem 5 [6, 7, 7] sts.
With RS facing, slip centre 19 [21, 23, 25] sts onto a
stitch holder, rejoin yarn to rem sts, K to end.
Complete to match first side reversing shapings.

FRONT

Work as given for Back until 12 [12, 12, 14] rows less
have been worked than on Back to shoulder shaping,
ending with RS facing for next row.
Shape neck
Next row – K14 [16, 19, 21], turn and work this side
first.
Work 1 row more.
Dec 1 st at neck edge on next 4 [5, 6, 7] rows.
10 [11, 13, 14] sts.
Cont straight until front matches Back to shoulder
shaping, ending with RS facing for next row.
Shape shoulder
Next row - Cast off 5 [5, 6, 7] sts, K to end.
Work 1 row more.
Cast off rem 5 [6, 7, 7] sts.
With RS facing, slip centre 17 sts onto a stitch holder,
rejoin yarn to rem sts, K to end.
Complete to match first side reversing shapings and
working 1 row more before shoulder shaping.

SLEEVES (Both alike)

Using 4mm (USA 6) needles and cast on 31 [33,
35, 37] sts.
Row 1 – (RS) * K1, P1, rep from * to last st, K1.
Row 2- P1, * K1, P1, rep from * to end.
These 2 rows form rib.
Work 3 rows more in rib.
Change to 4½mm (USA 7) needles
Beg with a P row cont in st st only shaping sides by
inc 1 st at each end of 4th and every foll 8th [8th,
10th, 10th] row to 47 [41, 51, 45] sts then on every foll

10th [10th, 12th, 12th] row to 49 [51, 53, 55] sts.
Cont straight until sleeve meas 33 [37, 41, 45]cm,
ending with RS facing for next row.
Shape top
Cast off 5 [5, 4, 3] sts at beg of next 2 rows.
39 [41, 45, 49] sts.
Dec 1 st at each end of next 3 rows. 33 [35, 39, 43] sts.
Work 1 row more.
Cast off 5 [5, 6, 7] sts at beg of next 2 rows.
23 [25, 27, 29] sts.
Cast off 4 [5, 6, 7] sts at beg of next 2 rows.
Cast off rem 15 sts.

MAKING UP
Join right shoulder seam

Neckband
With RS facing using 4mm (USA 6) needles pick up
and knit 11 [11, 11, 13] sts down left side of neck, K
across 17 sts left on a holder at front neck, pick up and
knit 11 [11, 11, 13] sts up right side of neck, 2 sts from
right side of back neck, K across 19 [21, 23, 25] sts left
on a holder at back neck and pick up and knit 3 sts
from left side of back neck.
63 [65, 67, 73] sts.
Beg with row 2 of rib as given for Sleeves, work 5 rows.
Cast off in rib.
Join left shoulder and neckband seam.
Join side and sleeve seams.
Insert sleeves.
Thread ribbon through eyelet holes.

33 [37:41:45] cm
(13 [14 1/2:16:18] in)

43 [45:47:49] cm
(17 [17 1/2:18 1/2:19 1/2] in)

35 [37.5: 39.5: 40.5] cm
(14 [15: 15 1/2: 16] in)

Quail
Marie Wallin

SIZE

	3/4	5/6	7/8	9/10	yrs

To fit chest

	55–57	59- 61	63 -67	69 - 73	cm

YARN
Rowan Calmer
Yarn A (Calmer 463)

	2	3	3	3	x 50g

Yarn B (Drift 460)

	1	2	2	2	x 50g

Yarn C (Calm 461)

	1	2	2	2	x 50g

Yarn D (Sugar 488)

	1	2	2	2	x 50g

Yarn E (Vintage 490)

	1	2	2	2	x 50g

NEEDLES
1 pair 4mm (no 8) (USA 6) needles
1 pair 5mm (no 6) (USA 8) needles
1 3.00mm (no11) (USA C2) crochet hook
5 x 00416 buttons

TENSION
21 sts and 30 rows to 10cm over st st on 5mm (USA 8) needles

CROCHET ABBREVIATIONS
ch = chain; dc = double crochet; tr = treble crochet;
ss = slip stitch.

Stripe sequence
Rows 1 and 2 – Yarn B
Rows 3 and 4 – Yarn C
Rows 5 and 6 – Yarn D
Rows 7 and 8 – Yarn E
Rows 9 and 10 – Yarn A

BACK
Using 4mm (USA 6) needles and yarn A, cast on
78 [82, 86, 90] sts.
Work 24 rows in g st.
Change to 5mm (USA 8) needles
Beg with a K row cont in st st, rep 10 row stripe
sequence until back meas 25 [25, 26, 27]cm, ending
with RS facing for next row.
Shape armholes
Keeping stripe sequence correct, cast off 6 [5, 4, 3] sts
at beg of next 2 rows. 66 [72, 78, 84] sts.
Dec 1 st at each end of next 3 rows, then 3 foll alt
rows. 54 [60, 66, 72] sts.
Cont straight until armhole meas 14.5 [16.5,
17.5, 18.5]cm, ending with RS facing for next row.
Shape shoulders and back neck
Next row – Keeping stripe sequence correct, cast off 5
[6, 7, 8] sts, K until there are 7 [8, 9, 10] sts on right
hand needle, turn and work this side first.
Next row – P2tog, P to end.
Cast off rem 6 [7, 8, 9] sts.
With RS facing rejoin yarn to rem sts, cast off centre
30 [32, 34, 36] sts, K to end.
Complete to match first side reversing shapings.

LEFT FRONT
Using 4mm (USA 6) needles and yarn A, cast on
39 [41, 43, 45] sts.
Work 24 rows in g st.
Change to 5mm (USA 8) needles
Beg with a K row cont in st st rep 10 row stripe
sequence, until left front matches Back to armhole
shaping, ending with RS facing for next row.
Shape armhole
Next row – Keeping stripe sequence correct, cast off 6
[5, 4, 3] sts, K to end. 33 [36, 39, 42] sts.
Work 1 row more.
Dec 1 st at armhole edge (beg) of next 3 rows, then
3 foll alt rows. 27 [30, 33, 36] sts.
Cont straight until 13 rows less have been worked
than on Back to shoulder shaping ending with WS
spacing for next row.
Shape neck
Next row – Cast off 5 [6, 7, 8] sts, P to end.
22 [24, 26, 28] sts.
Work 1 row more.
Next row – Cast off 6 sts, P to end. 16 [18, 20, 22] sts.
Work 1 row more.
Dec 1 st at beg of next 4 rows then on foll alt row.
11 [13, 15, 17] sts.
Cont until front matches Back to shoulder shaping,
ending with RS facing for next row.
Shape shoulder
Next Row - Cast off 5 [6, 7, 8] sts, K to end.

Work 1 row more.
Cast off rem 6 [7, 8, 9] sts.

RIGHT FRONT
Work to match Left Front, reversing shapings and working 1 row more before armhole and shoulder shaping and I row less before neck shaping.

SLEEVES (Both alike)
Using 4mm (USA 6) needles and yarn A, cast on 36 [40, 42, 44] sts.
Work 24 rows in g st.
Change to 5mm (USA 8) needles
Beg with a K row cont in st st rep 10 rows stripe sequence, shaping sides by inc 1 st at each end of next and every foll 6th [6th, 6th, 8th] row to 62 [60, 62, 70] sts.

Sizes 5/6 and 7/8 yrs only
Inc 1 st at each end of every foll 8th row to – [66, 68, –] sts.

All sizes
Cont straight until sleeve meas 32 [36, 40, 45]cm, ending with RS facing for next row.
Shape top
Keeping stripe sequence correct, cast off 6 [5, 4, 3] sts at beg of next 2 rows. 50 [56, 60, 64] sts.
Dec 1 st at each end of next 8 rows. 34 [40, 44, 48] sts.
Cast off 6 [9, 11, 13] sts at beg of next 2 rows.

Cast off rem 22 sts.

MAKING UP
Join side, shoulder and sleeve seams. Insert sleeves.
Crochet edging
With RS facing, using yarn C and 3.00mm (USA C2) crochet hook, beg at bottom edge of right front :-
Base row – 1ch, work dcs evenly up right front edge, around neck and down left front edge, working more or less dcs to ensure that work lies flat, turn.
Next row – 1ch, 1dc into each dc to end, working more or less dcs to ensure that work lies flat, fasten off.
Next row – With RS facing join in yarn E, 3ch, 2tr into next dc, miss 1dc, 1dc into next dc, miss 1dc, * 5tr into next dc, miss 1 dc, 1dc into next 1dc, miss 1dc, rep from * to end. Fasten off.
Large flower (make 3)
Using 3.00mm (USA C2) crochet hook and yarn E, make 6ch, ss into 1st ch to form a ring.
Round 1 – 1ch, 12dc into ring, ss to first dec, fasten off.
Round 2 – Join in yarn B, * 14ch, 1dc into next dc, rep from * 11 times more, ss into last dc, fasten off.
Small flower (make 4)
Using 3.00mm (USA C2) crochet hook and yarn C, make 4ch, 1dc into 1st ch to form a ring.
Round 1 – 1ch, 8dc into ring, ss to first dc, fasten off.
Round 2 – Join in yarn D, * 10ch, 1dc into next dc, rep from * 7 times more, ss into last dc, fasten off.
Attach flowers using photograph as a guide.
Sew on buttons.

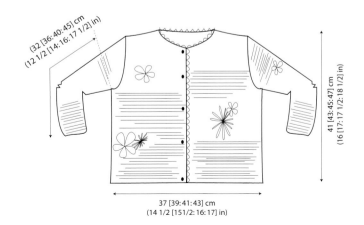

(32 [36:40:45] cm
(12 1/2 [14:16:17 1/2] in)

41 [43:45:47] cm
(16 [17:17 1/2:18 1/2] in)

37 [39:41:43] cm
(14 1/2 [151/2:16:17] in)

Duckling
Sarah Hatton

SIZE

	3/4	5/6	7/8	9/10	yrs

To fit chest

	55–57	59–61	63–67	69–73	cm

YARN

Rowan Cotton Glace (Oyster 730)

	9	10	11	13	x 50g

NEEDLES

1 pair 3mm (no11) (USA 3) needles
1 pair 2¾mm (no12) (USA 2) needles
2 x 00417 buttons
Scraps of yarn in contrast colours for embroidery

TENSION

28 sts and 38 rows to 10cm over st st on 3mm (USA 3) needles

LEFT FRONT

Using 3mm (USA 3) needles cast on 88 [90, 93, 96] sts.
Beg with a K row cont in st st dec 1 st at side edge (beg) in 13th [19th, 25th, 35th] and 4 foll 6th rows. 83 [85, 88, 91] sts.
Work 9 rows straight.
Inc 1 st at side edge in next and foll 6th row. 85 [87, 90, 93] sts.
Work 1 row more.
Work 32 rows inc 1 st at side edge in 5th and 3 foll 6th rows at same time dec 1 st at front edge in every row. 57 [59, 62, 65] sts.

Shape armhole

Next row – Cast off 6 [5, 4, 3] sts, K to last 2 sts, K2tog. 50 [53, 57, 61] sts.
Work 1 row more.
Dec 1 st at armhole edge (beg) in next 5 rows, then 3 foll alt rows at same time dec 1 st at front edge in next and every foll alt row. 36 [39, 43, 47] sts.
Dec1 st at front edge only in every foll alt row to 23 [26, 30, 34] sts.
Work 1 row ending with RS facing for next row.

Lace panel

Work 8 rows from chart A, dec 1 st at neck edge in next and every foll alt row. 19 [22, 26, 30] sts.

Cont in st st dec 1 st at neck edge in next and every foll alt row to 15 [17, 20, 22] sts.
Cont straight until armhole meas 15.5 [16.5, 17.5, 18.5] cm, ending with RS facing for next row.

Shape shoulder

Next row – Cast off 7 [8, 10, 11] sts, K to end.
Work 1 row more.
Cast off rem 8 [9, 10, 11] sts.

RIGHT FRONT

Using 3mm (USA 3) needles cast on 88 [90, 93, 96] sts.

Lace panel

Work 16 rows in patt foll chart B dec 1 [0, 0, 0] st at end of 13th [0, 0, 0] row. 87 [90, 93, 96] sts.
Beg with a K row cont in st st shaping side by dec 1 st at side edge (end) in 3rd [3rd, 9th, 19th] and 3 [4, 4, 4] foll 6th rows. 83 [85, 88, 91] sts.
Work 9 rows straight.
Inc 1 st at side edge in next and foll 6th row.
85 [87, 90, 93] sts.
Work 1 row more.
Work 32 rows inc 1 st at side edge in 5th and 3 foll 6th rows at same time dec 1 st at front edge in every row. 57 [59, 62, 65] sts.
Work to match Left front reversing shapings, working 1 row more before armhole and shoulder shaping and omitting the lace panel.

BACK

Using 3mm (USA 3) needles cast on 97 [101, 107, 113] sts.
Beg with a K row cont in st st shaping sides by dec 1 st at each end of 13th [19th, 25th, 35th] and 4 foll 6th rows. 87 [91, 97, 103] sts.
Work 9 rows straight.
Inc 1 st at each end of next and 5 foll 6th rows. 99 [103, 109, 115] sts.
Cont straight until back matches Fronts to armhole shaping, ending with RS facing for next row.

Shape armholes

Cast off 6 [5, 4, 3] sts at beg of next 2 rows. 87 [93, 101, 109] sts.
Dec 1 st at each end of next 5 rows, then 3 foll alt rows. 71 [77, 85, 93] sts.
Cont straight until back matches Left front to Lace

Chart A

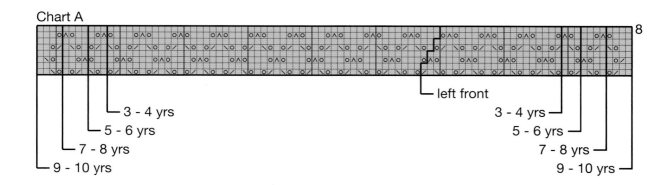

left front

3 - 4 yrs
5 - 6 yrs
7 - 8 yrs
9 - 10 yrs

3 - 4 yrs
5 - 6 yrs
7 - 8 yrs
9 - 10 yrs

Chart B

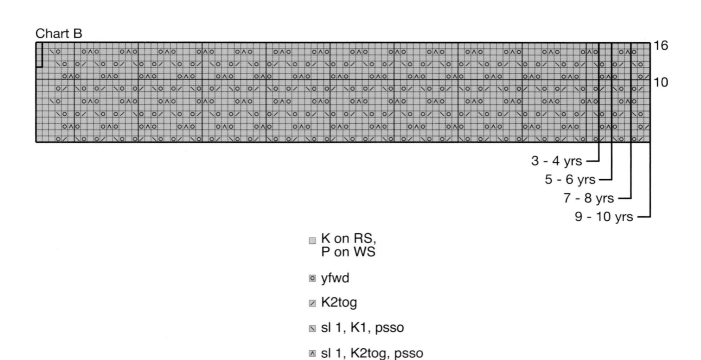

3 - 4 yrs
5 - 6 yrs
7 - 8 yrs
9 - 10 yrs

☐ K on RS,
   P on WS

⊡ yfwd

◩ K2tog

◪ sl 1, K1, psso

◮ sl 1, K2tog, psso

panel, ending with RS facing for next row.

Lace panel

Work 8 rows from chart A.

Cont straight until Back matches Left front to
shoulder shaping, ending with RS facing for next row.

Shape shoulders

Next row – Cast off 7 [8, 10, 11] sts, K until there are
11 [12, 13, 14] sts on right hand needle, turn and work
this side first.

Next row – Cast off 3 sts, P to end.

Cast off rem 8 [9, 10, 11] sts.

With RS facing rejoin yarn to rem sts, cast off centre
35 [37, 39, 43] sts, K to end.

Complete to match first side reversing shapings.

SLEEVES (Both alike)

Using 3mm (USA 3) needles cast on 51 [53, 55, 59] sts.

Knit 3 rows, ending with WS facing for next row.

Next row – (WS) K0 [1, 2, 4], (K2, inc in next st, K1,
inc in next st) 5 times, K1, (inc in next st, K1, inc in
next st, K2) 5 times, K0 [1, 2, 4]. 71 [73, 75, 79] sts.

Beg with a K row, work 6 rows in st st, ending with RS
facing for next row.

Lace panel

Work 8 rows in lace patt following chart C.

Cont in st st shaping sides by dec 1 st at each end of
3rd and every foll 6th row to 57 [59, 61, 65] sts.

Work 15 rows straight, ending with RS facing for next
row.

Inc 1 st at each end of next and every foll 4th [6th,
8th, 10th] row to 75 [77, 79, 83] sts.

Cont straight until sleeve meas 32 [36, 40, 45]cm,
ending with RS facing for next row.

Shape top

Cast off 6 [5, 4, 3] sts at beg of next 2 rows.

63 [67, 71, 77] sts.

Dec 1 st at each end of next 12 rows.

39 [43, 47, 53] sts.

Cast off 9 [11, 13, 16] sts at beg of next 2 rows.

Cast off rem 21 sts.

MAKING UP

Join side and shoulder seams.

Bottom edging

With RS facing using 2¾mm (USA 2) needles pick up
and knit 189 [193, 203, 211] sts all around bottom edge.

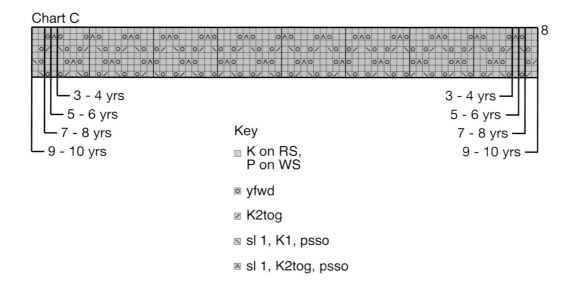

Chart C

8

3 - 4 yrs
5 - 6 yrs
7 - 8 yrs
9 - 10 yrs

3 - 4 yrs
5 - 6 yrs
7 - 8 yrs
9 - 10 yrs

Key

☐ K on RS,
P on WS

◉ yfwd

◩ K2tog

◩ sl 1, K1, psso

◪ sl 1, K2tog, psso

Knit 3 rows.

Next row - * Cast off 1 st, (take yarn round needle and draw loop through st on right hand needle as though to K a stitch) 4 times, cast off 1 st, rep from * to last st, fasten off.

Right button band

With RS facing using 2¾mm (USA 2) needles pick up and knit 47 [51, 57, 61] sts along straight edge of front and selvedge of bottom edging.

Knit 1 row.

Next row – K43 [47, 53, 57], cast off 2 sts, K to end.

Knit 1 row casting on 2 sts over 2 cast off sts on previous row.

Cast off as given for Bottom edging.

Left button band

With RS facing using 2¾mm (USA 2) needles pick up and knit 47[51, 57, 61] sts along selvedge of bottom edging and straight edge of front.

Knit 1 row.

Next row – K2, cast off 2 sts, K to end.

Knit 1 row casting on 2 sts over 2 cast off sts on previous row.

Cast off as given for Bottom edging.

Front edging

With RS facing using 2¾mm (USA 2) needles pick up and knit 89 [91, 93, 95] sts up shaped front edge, 41 [43, 45, 49] sts from back neck and 89 [91, 93, 95] sts down shaped front edge. 219 [225, 231, 239] sts.

Work as given for Bottom edging.

Join sleeve seams. Insert sleeves. Sew on buttons.

Work embroidery on right front following diagram.

Sew on buttons to match buttonholes.

32 [36: 40: 45] cm
(12 1/2 [14: 16: 17 1/2] in)

39.5 [42.5: 44.5: 48.5] cm
(15 1/2 [16 1/2: 17 1/2: 19] in)

35.5 [37: 39: 41] cm
(14 [14 1/2: 15 1/2: 16] in)

Peacock
Sarah Hatton

SIZE

	3/4	5/6	7/8	9/10	yrs

To fit chest

	55–57	59–61	63–67	69–73	cm

YARN
Rowan 4ply Cotton
Yarn A (Fresh 131)

	1	1	1	1	x 50g

Yarn B (Baby 141)

	1	1	1	1	x 50g

Yarn C (Cream153)

	3	3	4	5	x 50g

NEEDLES
1 pair 3¼mm (no 10) (USA 3) needles
Stitch holders
3 x 00416 buttons
1.2 metres of 0.5cm ribbon

TENSION
29 sts and 39 rows to 10cm over st st on 3¼mm
(USA 3) needles

BACK
Using 3¼mm (USA 3) needles and yarn A, cast on
145 [157, 163, 175] sts.
Edging
Row 1 – (RS) K1, * yfwd, K5, slip 2nd, 3rd, 4th and
5th of these sts over 1st st, yfwd, K1, rep from * to
end. 97 [105, 109, 117] sts.
Row 2 – Knit.
Using yarn B, K 1 row.
Row 4 – (WS) P1, * K1, P1, rep from * to end.
Row 5 - * K1, P1, rep from * to last st, K1.
Row 6 – As row 4.
These 6 rows form edging.
Using yarn A, knit 2 rows dec 1 [3, 1, 3] st evenly
across 2nd of these rows.
96 [102, 108, 114] sts.
Using yarn C proceed as follows:
Row 1 – (RS) Knit.
Row 2 – Purl.
Row 3 – As row 1.
Row 4 – As row 2.

Row 5 – K5 [2, 5, 2], * yfwd, Sl 1, K1, psso, K4, rep
from * to last 1 [4, 1, 4] sts, (yfwd, Sl 1, K1, psso) 0 [1,
0, 1] times, K1 [2, 1, 2].
Row 6 – Purl.
Rows 7 to 10 – As rows 1 to 4.
Row 11 – K2 [5, 2, 5], * yfwd, Sl 1, K1, psso, K4, rep
from * to last 4 [1, 4, 1] sts, (yfwd, Sl 1, K1, psso) 1 [0,
1, 0] time, K2 [1, 2, 1]
Row 12 – Purl.
These 12 rows form patt.
Keeping patt correct cont shaping sides by dec 1 st at
each end of 23rd and 2 foll 10th rows.
90 [96, 102, 108] sts.
Patt 7 [11, 15, 19] rows straight.
Waist band
Using yarn A, K 2 rows.
Using yarn B, proceed as follows:
Row 1 – (RS) Knit.
Row 2 – * P1, K1, rep from * to end.
Row 3 – K1, P1, * yfwd, K2tog, (K1, P1) twice, rep
from * to last 4 sts, yfwd, K2tog, K1, P1.
Row 4 – As row 2.
Using yarn A, K 2 rows.
Using yarn C, beg with a K row, cont in st st shaping
sides by inc 1 st at each end of 3rd and every foll
4th row to 98 [104, 110, 116] sts.
Cont straight until back meas 27 [28, 29, 30] cm,
ending with RS facing for next row.
Shape armholes
Cast off 5 [5, 3, 4] sts at beg of next 2 rows.
88 [94, 104, 108] sts.
Dec 1 st at each end of next 5 rows, then foll 2 alt
rows, then foll 4th row. 72 [78, 88, 92] sts.
Cont straight until armhole meas 15.5 [16.5,
17.5, 18.5]cm, ending with RS facing for next row.
Shape shoulders
Cast off 5 [5, 6, 7] sts at beg of next 2 rows.
62 [68, 76, 78] sts.
Next row – Cast off 5 [6, 7, 7] sts, K until there are
9 [10, 11, 11] sts on right hand needle, turn and work
this side first.
Next row – Cast off 4 sts, P to end.
Cast off rem 5 [6, 7, 7] sts.
With RS facing, cast off centre 34 [36, 40, 42] sts, patt
to end.
Complete to match first side reversing shapings.

LEFT FRONT

Using 3¼mm (USA 3) needles and yarn A, cast on 67 [73, 79, 85] sts.
Work 6 rows of edging as given for Back.
45 [49, 53, 57] sts.
Using yarn A, K 2 rows dec 0 [1, 2, 3] sts evenly across last of these rows. 45 [48, 51, 54] sts.
Using yarn C, proceed as follows:-
Row 1 - (RS) Knit.
Row 2 – Purl.
Row 3 – As row 1.
Row 4 – As row 2.
Row 5 – K5 [2, 5, 2], * yfwd, Sl 1, K1, psso, K4, rep from * to last 4 sts, yfwd, Sl 1, K1, psso, K2.
Row 6 – Purl.
Rows 7 to 10 – As rows 1 to 4.
Row 11 – K2 [5, 2, 5], * yfwd, Sl 1, K1, psso, K4, rep from * to last st, K1.
Row 12 – Purl.
These 12 rows form patt.
Keeping patt correct cont shaping sides by dec 1 st at side edge (beg) in 23rd and 2 foll 10th rows.
42 [45, 48, 51] sts.
Patt 7 [11, 15, 19] rows straight, inc 0 [3, 0, 3] sts evenly across last of these rows, ending with RS facing for next row. 42 [48, 48, 54] sts

** Waistband

Using yarn A, knit 2 rows.
Using yarn B, proceed as follows:-
Row 1 – Knit.
Row 2 - * P1, K1, rep from * to end.
Row 3 – K1, P1, * yfwd, K2tog, (K1, P1) twice, rep from * to last 4 sts, yfwd, K2tog, K1, P1.
Row 4 – As row 2.
Using yarn A, knit 2 rows, dec 0 [3, 0, 3] st evenly across last of these rows, 42 [45, 48, 51] sts.
Using yarn C, cont in st st shaping sides by inc 1 st at side edge in 3rd and every foll 4th row to 46 [49, 52, 55] sts.
Cont straight until left front matches Back to armhole shaping, ending with RS facing for next row.

Shape armhole

Next row - Cast off 5 [5, 3, 4] sts, K to end.
41 [44, 49, 51] sts.
Work 1 row more.
Dec 1 st at armhole edge in next 5 rows, then 2 foll alt rows, then foll 4th row. 33 [36, 41, 43] sts.
Cont straight until 27 rows less have been worked than on Back to shoulder shaping, ending with WS facing for next row.

Shape neck

Next row – Cast off 6 [7, 9, 10] sts, P to end.
27 [29, 32, 33] sts.
Dec 1 st at neck edge in next 3 rows, then on foll 9 alt rows. 15 [17, 20, 21] sts.
Cont straight until left front matches back to shoulder shaping, ending with RS facing for next row.

Shape shoulder

Cast off 5 [5, 6, 7] sts at beg of next and 5 [6, 7, 7] sts at beg of foll alt row.
Work 1 row more.
Cast off rem 5 [6, 7, 7] sts.

RIGHT FRONT

Using 3¼mm needles and yarn A, cast on 67 [73, 79, 85] sts.
Work 6 rows of edging as given for Back.
45 [49, 53, 57] sts.
Using yarn A, K 2 rows dec 0 [1, 2, 3] sts evenly across last of these rows. 45 [48, 51, 54] sts.
Using yarn C, proceed as follows:-
Row 1 – (RS) Knit.
Row 2 – Purl.
Row 3 – As row 1.
Row 4 – As row 2.
Row 5 – K2, * yfwd, Sl 1, K1, psso, K4, rep from * to last 1 [4, 1, 4] sts,
(yfwd, Sl 1, K1, psso,) 0 [1, 0, 1] times, K1 [2, 1, 2].
Row 6 – Purl.
Rows 7 to 10 – As rows 1 to 4.
Row 11 – K5 , * yfwd, Sl 1, K1, psso, K4, rep from * to last 4 [1, 4, 1] sts, (yfwd, Sl1, K1, psso) 1 [0, 1, 0] times, K2 [1, 2, 1].
Row 12 – Purl.
These 12 rows form patt.
Cont in patt shaping sides by dec 1 st at side edge (end) in 23rd and 2 foll 10th rows.
42 [45, 48, 51] sts.
Patt 7 [11, 15, 19] rows straight inc 0 [3, 0, 3] sts evenly across last of these rows and ending with RS facing for next row. 42 [48, 48, 54] sts.
Work as given for Left Front from ** reversing

shapings and working 1 row less before armhole and shoulder shaping and 1 row more before neck shaping.

SLEEVES (Both alike)
Using 3¼mm (USA 3) needles and yarn A, cast on 127 [133, 133, 139] sts.
Work 6 rows of edging as given for Back.
Using yarn A knit 2 rows dec 1 [3, 1, 3] sts evenly across last of these rows. 84 [86, 88, 90] sts.
Shape top
Using yarn C, proceed as follows:-
Row 1 – (RS) Cast off 5 [5, 3, 4] sts, K6 [4, 4, 4], * yfwd Sl 1, K1, psso, K4, rep from * to last 7 [5, 3, 4] sts, K7 [5, 3, 4]. 79 [81, 85, 86] sts.
Row 2 – Cast off 5 [5, 3, 4] sts, P to end. 74 [76, 82, 82] sts.
These 2 rows start shaping and set patt.
Keeping patt correct dec 1 st at each end of next 12 [14, 16, 18] rows. 50 [48, 50, 46] sts.
Cast off 16 [15, 16, 14] sts at beg of next 2 rows.
Cast off rem 18 sts.

MAKING UP
Join shoulder seams.
Neck edging
With RS facing using 3¼mm (USA 3) needles and yarn A, pick up and knit 30 sts up right side of neck, 41 [43, 45, 47] sts from back neck and 30 sts down left side of neck. 101 [103, 105, 107] sts.
Row 1 – (WS) Knit.
Using yarn B, knit 1 row.
Row 3 – P1, * K1, P1, rep from * to end.
Row 4 - * K1, P1, rep from * to last st, K1.
Row 5 – As row 3.
Using yarn A, K 1 row. Cast off.

Left front edging
With RS facing using 3¼mm (USA 3) needles and yarn A, pick up and knit 99 [107, 115, 121] sts evenly along neckband edge, front edge and rib edge.
Work as given for Neck edging.
Mark positions of buttons 1st to be 1cm from neck edge, 3rd to be 5cm above waistband and 2nd to be halfway between.
Right front edging
Work as given for Left front edging working buttonholes on row 4 to correspond with markers by working yfwd, K2tog.
Join side and sleeve seams.
Insert sleeves.
Sew on buttons. Thread ribbon through eyelet holes at waist.

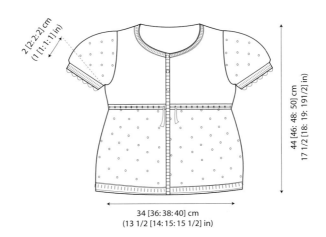

2 [2: 2: 2] cm
(1 [1: 1: 1] in)

44 [46: 48: 50] cm
17 1/2 [18: 19: 191/2] in)

34 [36: 38: 40] cm
(13 1/2 [14: 15: 15 1/2] in)

Information

Tension

Obtaining the correct tension is perhaps the single factor which can make the difference between a successful garment and a disastrous one. It controls both the shape and size of an article, so any variation, however slight, can distort the finished garment. Different designers feature in our books and it is their tension, given at the start of each pattern, which you must match. We recommend that you knit a square in pattern and/or stocking stitch (depending on the pattern instructions) of perhaps 5 - 10 more stitches and 5 - 10 more rows than those given in the tension note. Mark out the central 10cm square with pins. If you have too many stitches to 10cm try again using thicker needles, if you have too few stitches to 10cm try again using finer needles. Once you have achieved the correct tension your garment will be knitted to the measurements indicated in the size diagram shown at the end of the pattern.

Sizing & Size Diagram Note

The instructions are given for the smallest size. Where they vary, work the figures in brackets for the larger sizes. One set of figures refers to all sizes. Included with most patterns in this magazine is a 'size diagram', or sketch of the finished garment and its dimensions. To help you choose the size of garment to knit please refer to the NEW sizing guide on page 159.

Chart Note

Many of the patterns in the book are worked from charts. Each square on a chart represents a stitch and each line of squares a row of knitting. Each colour used is given a different letter and these are shown in the materials section, or in the key alongside the chart of each pattern. When working from the charts, read odd rows (K) from right to left and even rows (P) from left to right, unless otherwise stated.

Knitting With Colour

There are two main methods of working colour into a knitted fabric: Intarsia and Fairisle techniques. The first method produces a single thickness of fabric and is usually used where a colour is only required in a particular area of a row and does not form a repeating pattern across the row, as in the fairisle technique.

Intarsia: The simplest way to do this is to cut short lengths of yarn for each motif or block of colour used in a row. Then joining in the various colours at the appropriate point on the row, link one colour to the next by twisting them around each other where they meet on the wrong side to avoid gaps. All ends can then either be darned along the colour join lines, as each motif is completed or then can be " knitted-in" to the fabric of the knitting as each colour is worked into the pattern. This is done in much the same way as"weaving- in" yarns when working the Fairisle technique and does save time darning-in ends. It is essential that the tension is noted for Intarsia as this may vary from the stocking stitch if both are used in the same pattern.

Fair isle type knitting: When two or three colours are worked repeatedly across a row, strand the yarn not in use loosely behind the stitches being worked. If you are working with more than two colours, treat the "floating" yarns as if they were one yarn and always spread the stitches to their correct width to keep them elastic. It is advisable not to carry the stranded or "floating" yarns over more than three stitches at a time, but to weave them under and over the colour you are working. The "floating" yarns are therefore caught at the back of the work.

Finishing Instructions

After working for hours knitting a garment, it seems a great pity that many garments are spoiled because such little care is taken in the pressing and finishing process. Follow the following tips for a truly professional-looking garment.

Pressing

Block out each piece of knitting and following the instructions on the ball band press the garment pieces, omitting the ribs. Tip: Take special care to press the edges, as this will make sewing up both easier and neater. If the ball band indicates that the fabric is not to be pressed, then covering the blocked out fabric with a damp white cotton cloth and leaving it to stand will have the desired effect. Darn in all ends neatly along the selvage edge or a colour join, as appropriate.

Stitching

When stitching the pieces together, remember to match areas of colour and texture very carefully where they meet. Use a seam stitch such as back stitch or mattress stitch for all main knitting seams and join all ribs and neckband with mattress stitch, unless otherwise stated.

Construction

Having completed the pattern instructions, join left shoulder and neckband seams as detailed above. Sew the top of the sleeve to the body of the garment using the method detailed in the pattern, referring to the appropriate guide:

Straight cast-off sleeves: Place centre of cast-off edge of sleeve to shoulder seam. Sew top of sleeve to body, using markers as guidelines where applicable.

Square set-in sleeves: Place centre of cast-off edge of sleeve to shoulder seam. Set sleeve head into armhole, the straight sides at top of sleeve to form a neat right-angle to cast-off sts at armhole on back and front.

Shallow set-in sleeves: Place centre of cast off edge of sleeve to shoulder seam. Match decreases at beg of armhole shaping to decreases at top of sleeve. Sew sleeve head into armhole, easing in shapings.

Set- in sleeves: Place centre of cast-off edge of sleeve to shoulder seam. Set in sleeve, easing sleeve head into armhole.

Join side and sleeve seams.

Slip stitch pocket edgings and linings into place. Sew on buttons to correspond with buttonholes. Ribbed welts and neckbands and any areas of garter stitch should not be pressed.

Working a Lace Pattern

When working a lace pattern it is important to remember that if you are unable to work both the increase and corresponding decrease and vica versa, the stitches should be worked in stocking stitch.

Embroidery Diagrams

Lazy Daisy

Cross Stitch

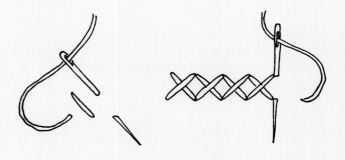

French Knot

Abbreviations

K	knit
P	purl
st(s)	stitch(es)
inc	increas(e)(ing)
dec	decreas(e)(ing)
st st	stocking stitch (1 row K , 1 row P)
g st	garter stitch (K every row)
beg	begin(ning)
foll	following
rem	remain(ing)
rev st st	reverse stocking stitch (1 row K , 1 row P)
rep	repeat
alt	alternate
cont	continue
patt	pattern
tog	together
mm	millimetres
cm	centimetres
in(s)	inch(es)
RS	right side
WS	wrong side
sl 1	slip one stitch
psso	pass slipped stitch over
p2sso	pass 2 slipped stitches over
tbl	through back of loop
M1	make one stitch by picking up horizontal loop before next stitch and knitting into back of it
M1P	make one stitch by picking up horizontal loop before next stitch and purling into back of it
yfwd	yarn forward
yrn	yarn round needle
meas	measures
0	no stitches, times or rows
-	no stitches, times or rows for that size
yon	yarn over needle
yrn	yarn round needle
wyib	with yarn at back

Crochet Terms

UK crochet terms and abbreviations have been used throughout. The list below gives the US equivalent where they vary.

Abbrev.	UK	US
dc	double crochet	single crochet
htr	half treble	half double crochet
tr	treble	double crochet
dtr	double treble	treble
ttr	triple treble	double treble
qtr	quadruple treble	triple treble

= Easy, straight forward knitting

= Suitable for the average knitter

= For the more experienced knitter

Rowan Children's Sizing Guide

When you knit and wear a Rowan children's design we want you to be happy with the look and feel of the finished garment. This all starts with the size and fit of the design you choose. To help you to achieve the correct fit for your child, we have looked at the sizing of our children's patterns. This has resulted in the introduction of the sizing guide below.

Dimensions in the charts below are body measurements, not garment dimensions, therefore please refer to the measuring guide to help you to determine which is the best size for your child.

Measuring Guide

For maximum comfort and to ensure the correct fit when choosing the size to knit, please follow the tips below when checking the size of your child.

Measure your child close to the body over their underwear, but don't pull the tape measure too tight!

- **Chest** – measure around the fullest part of the chest and across the shoulder blades.

- **Waist** – measure around the natural waistline, just above the hip bone.

- **Hips** – measure around the fullest part of the bottom

If you don't wish to measure your child, note the size of their favourite jumper that you like the fit of. Our sizes are now comparable to the clothing sizes from the major high street retailers, so if their favourite jumper is an age 3/4, then our age 3 – 4 yrs should be approximately the same fit.

To be extra sure, measure their favourite jumper and then compare these measurements with the Rowan size diagram given at the end of the individual instructions.

Finally, once you have decided which size is best for you to knit, please ensure that you achieve the tension required for the design.

Remember if your tension is too loose, your garment will be bigger than the pattern size and you may use more yarn. If your tension is too tight, your garment could be smaller than the pattern size and you will have yarn left over.

Furthermore if your tension is incorrect, the handle of your fabric will be too stiff or floppy and will not fit properly. It really does make sense to check your tension before starting every project.

Standard Sizing Guide for Children

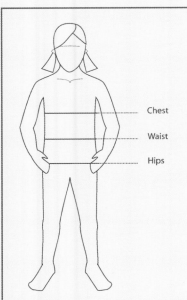

The sizing within this chart are based on the larger size within the range, ie. age 3 – 4 yrs will be based on age 4 yrs.

AGE	3-4 yrs	5-6yrs	7-8 yrs	9-10 yrs	
To fit height	38.5 – 41	43.25 – 45.5	48 – 50.25	52.75 – 55	(in)
	98 – 104	110 – 116	122 – 128	134 – 140	(cm)
To fit chest	21.5 – 22.5	23 – 24	25 – 26.5	27 – 28.75	(in)
	55 – 57	59 – 61	63 – 67	69 – 73	(cm)
To fit waist	21 – 21.25	21.5 – 22.25	23 – 23.75	24 – 25	(in)
	53 – 54	55 – 57	58 – 60	61 – 64	(cm)
To fit hips	23 – 23.75	24.5 – 25.5	26.75 - 28	28.75 – 30.75	(in)
	58 – 60	62 – 65	68 – 71	73 – 78	(cm)

Chest

Waist

Hips

Stockists

AUSTRALIA: Australian Country Spinners, 314 Albert Street, Brunswick, Victoria 3056
Tel: (61) 3 9380 3888
Fax: (61) 3 9387 2674
E-mail: sales@auspinners.com.au

AUSTRIA: Coats Harlander GmbH, Autokaderstrasse 31, A -1210 Wien.
Tel: (01) 27716 – 0
Fax : (01) 27716 - 228

BELGIUM: Pavan, Meerlaanstraat 73, B9860 Balegem (Oosterzele).
Tel: (32) 9 221 8594
Fax: (32) 9 221 8594
E-mail: pavan@pandora.be

CANADA: Diamond Yarn, 9697 St Laurent, Montreal, Quebec, H3L 2N1
Tel: (514) 388 6188

Diamond Yarn (Toronto), 155 Martin Ross, Unit 3, Toronto, Ontario, M3J 2L9
Tel: (416) 736 6111
Fax: (416) 736 6112
E-mail: diamond@diamondyarn.com
Internet: www.diamondyarn.com

CHINA: Coats Shanghai Ltd, No 9 Building , Baosheng Road, Songjiang Industrial Zone, Shanghai.
Tel: (86- 21) 5774 3733
Fax: (86-21) 5774 3768

DENMARK: Coats Danmark A/S, Nannasgade 28, 2200 Kobenhavn N.
Tel: (45) 35 86 90 50
Fax: (45) 35 82 15 10
E-mail: info@hpgruppen.dk
Internet: www.hpgruppen.dk

FINLAND: Coats Opti Oy, Ketjutie 3, 04220 Kerava
Tel: (358) 9 274 871
Fax: (358) 9 2748 7330
E-mail: coatsopti.sales@coats.com

FRANCE: Coats France/Steiner Frères, 100, avenue du Général de Gaulle, 18 500 Mehun-Sur-Yèvre
Tel: (33) 02 48 23 12 30
Fax: (33) 02 48 23 12 40

GERMANY: Coats GMbH, Kaiserstrasse 1, D-79341 Kenzingen
Tel: (49) 7644 8020
Fax: (49) 7644 802399 Internet: www.coatsgmbh.de

HOLLAND: de Afstap, Oude Leliestraat 12, 1015 AW Amsterdam
Tel: (31) 20 6231445
Fax: (31) 20 427 8522

HONG KONG:
Coats China Holdings Ltd, 19/F Millennium City 2, 378 Kwun Tong Road, Kwun Tong, Kowloon
Tel: (852) 2798 6886
Fax: (852) 2305 0311

ICELAND: Storkurinn, Laugavegi 59, 101 Reykjavik
Tel: (354) 551 8258
E-mail: malin@mmedia.is

ITALY: D.L. srl, Via Piave, 24 – 26, 20016 Pero, Milan
Tel: (39) 02 339 10 180
Fax: (39) 02 33914661

JAPAN: Puppy-Jardin Co Ltd, 3-8-11 Kudanminami Chiyodaku, Hiei Kudan Bldg. 5F, Tokyo
Tel: (81) 3 3222-7076
Fax: (81) 3 3222- 7066
E-mail: info@rowan-jaeger.com

KOREA: Coats Korea Co Ltd, 5F Kuckdong B/D, 935-40 Bangbae- Dong, Seocho-Gu, Seoul
Tel: (82) 2 521 6262.
Fax: (82) 2 521 5181

LEBANON: y.knot, Saifi Village, Mkhalissiya Street 162, Beirut, Tel: (961) 1 992211. Fax: (961) 1 315553.
E-mail: y.knot@cyberia.net.lb

NEW ZEALAND: Please contact Rowan for details of stockists

NORWAY: Coats Knappehuset AS, Pb 100 Ulset, 5873 Bergen
Tel: (47) 55 53 93 00
Fax: (47) 55 53 93 93

SINGAPORE: Golden Dragon Store, 101 Upper Cross Street #02-51, People's Park Centre, Singapore 058357
Tel: (65) 6 5358454
Fax : (65) 6 2216278
E-mail: gdscraft@hotmail.com

SOUTH AFRICA: Arthur Bales PTY, PO Box 44644, Linden 2104
Tel: (27) 11 888 2401
Fax: (27) 11 782 6137

SPAIN: Oyambre, Pau Claris 145, 80009 Barcelona. Tel: (34) 670 011957
Fax: (34) 93 4872672
E-mail: oyambre@oyambreonline.com

SWEDEN: Coats Expotex AB, Division Craft, Box 297, 401 24 Goteborg
Tel: (46) 33 720 79 00
Fax: 46 31 47 16 50

SWITZERLAND: Coats Stroppel AG, CH -5300 Turgi (AG) .
Tel: (41) 562981220
Fax: (41) 56 298 12 50

TAIWAN:
Laiter Wool Knitting Co Ltd, 10-1 313 Lane, Sec 3, Chung Ching North Road, Taipei
Tel: (886) 2 2596 0269
Fax : (886) 2 2598 0619

U.S.A.: Westminster Fibers Inc, 4 Townsend West, Suite 8, Nashua, New Hampshire 03063
Tel: (1 603) 886 5041 / 5043
Fax (1 603) 886 1056
E-mail: rowan@westminsterfibers.com

U.K: Rowan, Green Lane Mill, Holmfirth, West Yorkshire, England HD9 2DX
Tel: +44 (0) 1484 681881
Fax: +44 (0) 1484 687920
E-mail: mail@knitrowan.com
Inernet: www.knitrowan.com

For stockists in all other countries please contact Rowan for details.